VOYAGING
TO
CATHAY

Jacquard coverlet, about 1840. COLLECTIONS OF GREENFIELD VILLAGE AND THE HENRY FORD MUSE[...]

ALFRED TAMARIN
and
SHIRLEY GLUBOK

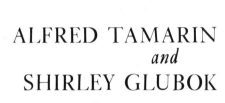

The Viking Press ❧ *New York*

VOYAGING TO CATHAY

Americans in the China Trade

Book design by Lucy Bitzer

LIBRARY OF CONGRESS CATALOGING IN PUBLICATION DATA

Tamarin, Alfred
  Voyaging to Cathay: Americans in the China Trade

  SUMMARY: Traces the earliest contacts between the
United States and China from the years following the
American Revolution until the advent of the steamship.
  1. United States—Commerce—China—History—Juve-
nile literature. 2. China—Commerce—United States—His-
tory—Juvenile literature. [1. United States—Commerce—
China—History. 2. China—Commerce—United States—
History] I. Glubok, Shirley, joint author. II. Title.
HF3120.T35   382'.0973'051   75–14415
ISBN 0–670–74857–9

ACKNOWLEDGMENTS

The authors gratefully acknowledge the kind assistance of
Paul Molitar, Jr., Director, Museum of the American China Trade;
Nobuko Kajitani, Associate Conservator, The Metropolitan Museum
of Art; Clare Le Corbeiller, Associate Curator of Western European Arts, The Metropolitan Museum of Art; John A. Pope, former
Director, Freer Gallery of Art; and especially the helpful cooperation
of Francis R. Carpenter, Associate Director, Museum of the American China Trade.

American mariner, oil painting by unknown American artist, 1804
COURTESY, MUSEUM OF THE AMERICAN CHINA TRADE, MILTON, MASS.

PREFACE

The stories of America's early experiences in the China trade can still fill us with excitement almost two centuries later. We admire the brave young men who dared unknown seas in small ships to reach the opposite ends of the world, keeping open vital commercial lifelines for the new American nation. We remember youthful seamen and traders who gambled their lives and their fortunes and often lost both.

In an overall view of history, the American China trade was invaluable to the survival and growth of the new United States. More important than the exotic teas, silks, and porcelains which it provided were the outlets kept open for American farming and industry and the incentives created for the growth of shipbuilding, mining, canal building, and railroad construction. Trade with China and the Orient kept the nation's eyes turned toward the Pacific Ocean and provided a constant spur for America's expansion to the West. Relations between the United States and Canada were affected by the exploits of China traders.

But even though the China trade as a whole was of great historical importance, some aspects of it were thoughtless and cruel. How can there be admiration for the seamen and merchants who smuggled opium into China? How unnatural, in the light of present-day knowledge of ecology and the interdependence of all life, seems the behavior of men who slaughtered the otters and seals and cut down the sandalwood forests!

There is very little in print about the China trade for young people who wish to read further. A quick survey of Chinese civilization can be found in *China* by Hyman Kublin (Houghton Mifflin, 1972) and *Ancient China* by Richard L. Walker (Franklin Watts, 1972). *The First Book of China Clippers*, by Louise Dickinson Rich (Franklin Watts, 1962), touches briefly on some of the high spots of the China trade, and *Clipper Ships and Captains*, by Jane D. Lyon (American Heritage, 1962), begins where our story ends. Another kind of early trade, involving New England, is dealt with in *Rum, Slaves and Molasses* by Clifford Lindsey Alderman (Crowell-Collier Press, 1972). *Carry on Mr. Bowditch* by Jean Lee Latham (Houghton Mifflin, 1955) is the story of the navigator and captain from Salem.

Marco Polo's Adventures in China by Milton Rugoff (American Heritage, 1964) tells of one of the first, and perhaps the most famous, European visitor to the Far East. *Through the Vermillion Gates* by Eleanor C. Munro (Pantheon, 1971) describes China's ancient civilization as it was brought to light by modern discoveries. And finally, *The Art of China* and *The Art of the New American Nation*, both by Shirley Glubok (Macmillan, 1973 and 1972), describe masterpieces made in the Far East and in America at the time of our story.

Ship President Adams *wrecked on the coast of China,*
September 29, 1812. Painting by unknown Chinese artist
Courtesy, museum of the american china trade

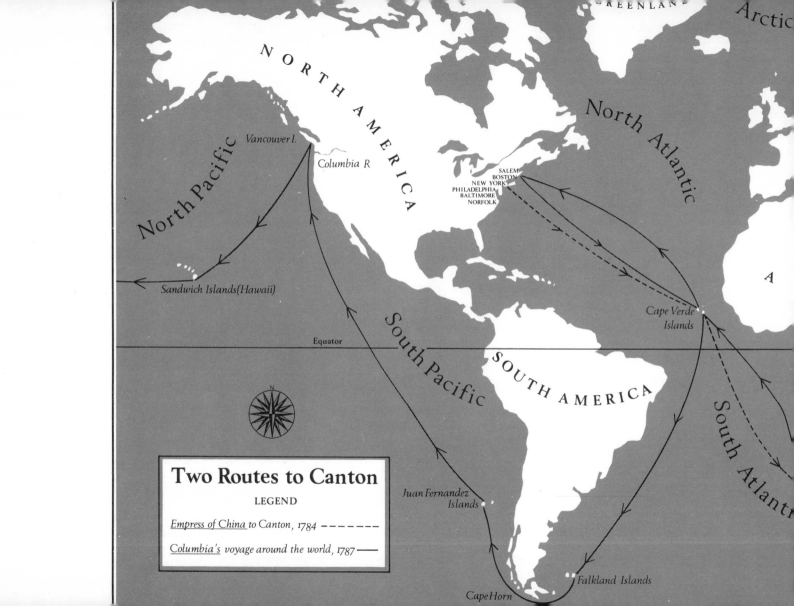

GREENLAND

Arctic

NORTH AMERICA

North Atlantic

North Pacific

Vancouver I.

Columbia R

SALEM
BOSTON
NEW YORK
PHILADELPHIA
BALTIMORE
NORFOLK

A

Sandwich Islands(Hawaii)

Cape Verde
Islands

Equator

South Pacific

SOUTH AMERICA

South Atlantic

Juan Fernandez
Islands

Two Routes to Canton

LEGEND

Empress of China to Canton, 1784 – – – – – –

Columbia's voyage around the world, 1787 ———

Falkland Islands

Cape Horn

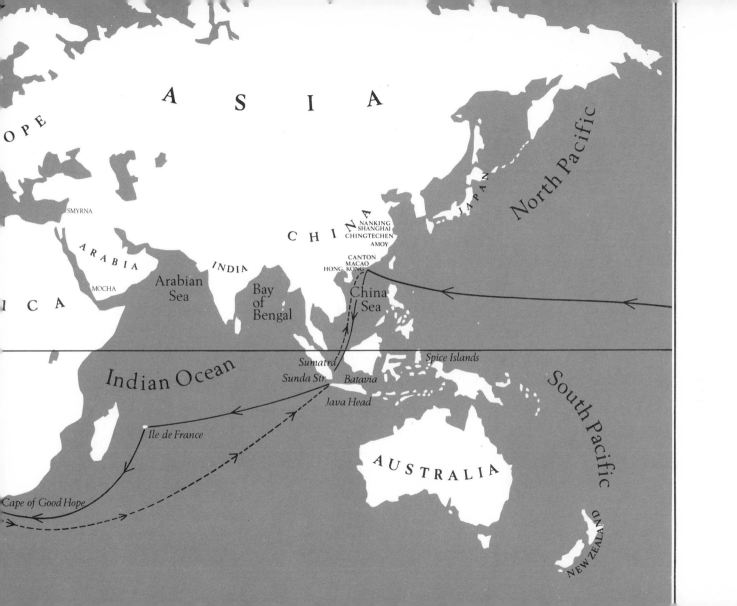

ASIA

EUROPE

SMYRNA

ARABIA

MOCHA

INDIA

Arabian
Sea

Bay
of
Bengal

CHINA

NANKING
SHANGHAI
CHINGTECHEN
AMOY

CANTON
MACAO
HONG KONG

China
Sea

JAPAN

North Pacific

AFRICA

Indian Ocean

Sumatra

Sunda Str.

Batavia

Spice Islands

Java Head

Ile de France

Cape of Good Hope

AUSTRALIA

South Pacific

NEW ZEALAND

Loading tea at Canton in 1855. Watercolor by Tingqua

CONTENTS

VOYAGING
TO
CATHAY

CHAPTER 1

The War for Independence Ends

For two days British warships in the harbor of New York strained at their anchors, waiting for a break in the weather so that the King's defeated troops could come on board. The time was November 1783. The English army, having lost the war for American independence, was leaving the city it had occupied for seven years.

Even in defeat Britain's red-coated soldiers could not resist flinging one last taunt at the oncoming Americans. Behind them the retreating troops left a British flag flying high in the wind from the top of a greased pole. The rope halyards used to raise and lower the flag had been cut to put them out of reach, and they slapped noisily against the slippery flagpole. By noon on November 25 the last of the British soldiers had clambered aboard the waiting ships.

All morning long the victorious American army had been waiting to move in and take possession of the city. With the British gone, patriotic New Yorkers came pouring into the streets to give George Washington and his troops a rousing welcome.

The British colors overhead did not fly long. Urged on by the encouraging shouts from the crowds, an American seaman tied metal cleats onto his boots and climbed the flagpole, slowly and painfully. He reached the dangling ropes and cut away the defeated enemy's flag. The onlookers in the street cheered.

Meanwhile the American troops moved into the city, marching behind General Washington, an impressive figure astride his horse. By three o'clock in the afternoon the victorious Americans were in complete control of New York. With Washington came General Henry Knox, the rotund commander of artillery. Among Gen-

George Washington: printed cotton handkerchief, 1775–1800

eral Knox's aides was a young, unknown major from Boston named Samuel Shaw.

Nine days after the British troops were gone, Washington could say farewell to his men. His heart filled with emotion as he took leave of the troops, with whom he had served so long, to return to his home at Mount Vernon.

Young Major Shaw, probably present on the historic occasion of Washington's leave-taking, would have waved good-bye to the tall figure of the Commander-in-Chief, disappearing in a small boat across New York Bay. That night Shaw did not yet know that he too would soon be making his own departure from the same harbor. Shaw's voyage would help strengthen America's new freedom by developing an independent trade with China.

With the British gone, the people of New York surveyed the wreckage of their city. During seven years of war many buildings had collapsed from neglect; others had been consumed by fires that had reduced much of

*Sailing ships at Mount Vernon: painting by unknown American artist,
early nineteenth century*

the city to ashes. The waterfront was desolate. Wharves, their wooden planking in disrepair, sagged into the rivers.

Other seaports along the Atlantic coast had also suffered from the war. Many had been occupied by British forces; others had been blockaded by the British navy.

In New England nothing was left of the fishing fleet. Some of the fishing boats had been captured or destroyed by the British. Others, too slow to be of any service during the war, had been dragged onto the beaches and left to rot. The few vessels that survived needed extensive repairs before they could put out to sea once again. Also gone were the whaling ships, which had totaled almost two hundred before the war. All but four or five had been lost, captured, or burned.

The war had also been devastating to American shipbuilders. For many years before the war Massachusetts alone had witnessed the launching of approximately one hundred and twenty-five vessels annually. But only forty-five ships went down the ways during the year after the end of the Revolutionary War, and some of them were so poorly constructed that no more orders came from European buyers. For two years, from 1785 to 1787, the shipyards were reduced to building only fifteen to twenty ships a year. The yards seemed almost empty and silent.

The first two years after the end of the War for Independence were times of deep depression. The war was over, but the new nation was still struggling to survive. The government of the defeated English king was in no mood to help its former colonies. English ports were closed to most American shipping, except for a few raw materials, such as pitch, turpentine, and tar. Trade between the British West Indies and the United States was forbidden, and the shipments of corn, dried fish, lumber, horses, and cattle, which had once been traded for coffee, cotton, rum, and indigo in the Caribbean islands, were ended. It was a drastic blow for American shipowners and shipbuilders. The effect on the British West Indies proved even more disastrous. When hurricanes destroyed the local crops, thousands died of starvation.

Building the frigate Philadelphia: *engraving by W. Birch and Son, 1800*

To make matters worse, America's recent wartime allies, France and Spain, also sealed their harbors to commerce from the United States. The owners of the few American ships that had survived the war were eager to send off their fleets. But to what destination? And carrying what cargo?

CHAPTER *2*

_____

An Unfinished Voyage

DURING THE ENTIRE time that Great Britain controlled the thirteen colonies, no American ship had been permitted to sail to China. All English trading with the Far East was monopolized by the British East India Company. American colonists could buy Oriental goods, such as tea, silk, and porcelain, but only from English merchants, who were supplied in turn by the "Honorable John Company," as the monopoly trading organization was slyly referred to. But now that the American Revolution was over, the China trade was opened to American ships.

During December 1783, soon after the British fleet had left New York, the *Harriet*, a tiny sloop from Hingham, Massachusetts, near Boston, headed out to sea. Her destination was the port of Canton in the empire of China on the other side of the globe. The 55-ton *Harriet* seemed hardly big enough to dare a voyage halfway around the world and back.

The *Harriet*'s first cargo, intended to launch America's trade with China, consisted of ginseng root. Ginseng is the common name of an aromatic root that was very much in demand in China. It existed in two species, one native to Manchuria and Korea, the other gathered in the cool woodlands along the Atlantic seaboard from Canada to Florida.

In China ginseng had been used for centuries as a

Ginseng root

medicine and a tonic. It was believed to be a cure-all, with miraculous healing properties—a remedy for many diseases, as well as a tonic to restore youth and vigor. Because many believed it could defer old age, ginseng was known as "the dose of immortality."

Among the folk tales about ginseng is the story of a Korean boy named Kim, whose aged father was dying. In despair Kim fasted and prayed to the spirits of the mountains. The spirits appeared in a dream and guided him to a hilly spot at the foot of a mountain near Manchuria, where he found a wild plant with white flowers and crimson fruit. The root of the plant was forked, resembling the shape of the human body. Kim brought home the ginseng root, which miraculously cured his father.

An ancient Chinese legend tells the story of a group of people who heard a mysterious voice calling to them night after night. The people searched everywhere for the source of the voice. Finally they dug into the ground where ginseng plants were growing. Five feet below the

Ships at anchor off the Cape of Good Hope: China trade porcelain for Dutch market, 1750–1760

surface they found roots that were shaped roughly like a human being with tiny arms and legs. They took the ginseng roots home and the strange voices were heard no more.

In China everything about ginseng involved elaborate ceremony. The root was placed in the smallest of a series of boxes nesting snugly inside one another. Between the boxes were paper packages, containing quicklime to keep the precious root dry. The tiniest of the receptacles, lined with lead, was covered with silver and wrapped in silk. If a visitor was permitted even a glimpse of the ginseng, he was politely asked to hold his breath so that the air would not be fouled and the power of the root weakened. No one was allowed to hold the ginseng or even to touch it.

Ginseng was prepared in the following manner: The root was set carefully in water in a silver vessel fitted inside a copper kettle. The silver vessel had a cup-like cover that was filled with rice. The space between the silver and copper walls was filled with water, which was heated to warm the ginseng and cook the rice. The tea-like brew that resulted was to be drunk at the same time that the boiled rice was eaten.

With its cargo of ginseng, gathered in the forests of New England, the *Harriet* set out from Boston harbor, her course set toward the southern tip of Africa. On the bridge was Captain Hallet, a veteran of the American Revolution, who had learned his navigating skills on a privateer. Privateers were privately owned ships which were officially commissioned by the government to capture British ships and their cargoes. All booty captured by a privateer became the property of the ship's owner.

Several weeks after Hallet left Boston, he put in at the Cape of Good Hope on the southern tip of Africa. There the little sloop found herself in the company of a hulking British East India merchantman, one of the large English vessels in the China trade, almost thirty times the size of the *Harriet*.

Despite the small capacity of the American ship, the Britishers saw a hint of troublesome competition in the young, vigorous seagoing New Englanders and decided to keep the Americans away from China. While still at anchor at the Cape of Good Hope, the British offered Hallet double the weight of *Harriet*'s ginseng in Chinese tea. The deal was profitable and Captain Hallet accepted, turned his ship around and set sail again, this time bound for home. The first American ship to set sail for China never reached her destination.

CHAPTER *3*

The Empress of China Sails Away

On February 22, 1784, George Washington's fifty-second birthday, a reconverted privateer slipped away from a wharf in New York harbor and headed out to sea on what would prove to be an historic journey.

The ship had seen duty as a sea raider in the War for Independence. Now she had been refitted and given a new name, one suited to her role as a commercial trader: the *Empress of China*.

The "handsome, commodious, and elegant ship," as the vessel was described, moved slowly down the bay, her copper-sheathed hull glistening in the sun. The cannon that the ship had carried during her war years had been left undisturbed, and parts of her hull were still covered with armor plate. It was quite possible that the ship would need the arms and armor to ward off attacks by pirates in the eastern seas.

As the *Empress of China* moved seaward, her cannon fired a thirteen-gun, or "Federal," salute in farewell. Shore batteries replied with twelve guns, wishing Godspeed to the departing vessel.

Aboard the ship, for the short run out of the harbor, were the ship's owners and friends of the officers. Among them was Robert Morris of Philadelphia, the main sponsor of the voyage, who had been one of the major financial backers of the American Revolution. Morris, who had once made a fortune in trade with the West Indies, now hoped to recover from some heavy wartime losses. His partner in the venture was Daniel Parker and Company of New York. The ship and its cargo represented a total investment of $120,000.

Off Sandy Hook, at the mouth of the harbor, the leave-taking ended. All the well-wishers returned to shore while the *Empress of China*, her sails spread, headed into the Atlantic winds. The ship's course was south and east. Her destination was the only port in China open to foreign shipping—Canton.

The captain of the ship was John Green, a veteran sea officer, who had served aboard an American privateer. His crew consisted of three other officers, a surgeon and a surgeon's mate, a purser, two midshipmen, a clerk and thirty-four seamen. The ship's complement included two carpenters, a cooper to make and repair barrels, and several cabin boys. There was also a gunner in charge of the ten cannon stored below deck.

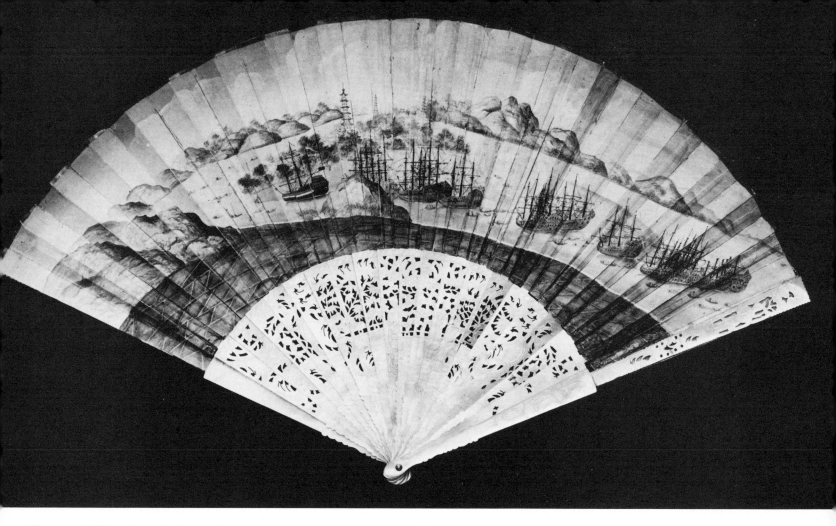

Empress of China *fan: painting on ivory, 1785*

Samuel Shaw

The business affairs of the trading voyage were the responsibility of a supercargo, who was in charge of the commercial interests of the voyage. The supercargo of the *Empress of China* was Samuel Shaw, who had come to New York just a few months earlier as the wartime aide of General Knox. Barely three weeks after Shaw and his fellow officers had said good-bye to George Washington, the young major announced his decision to seek his fortune in eastern seas. As his assistant went his wartime companion, Thomas Randall.

The first cargo on an American ship to China consisted mostly of ginseng. After almost 30 tons of it had been put on board, the remainder of the ship was filled with 1270 woolen garments, known as camlets, 316 piculs of cotton (1 picul equals 133⅓ pounds), and 2600 fur skins. Furs were known to be in demand in China to make warm garments for the cold winters. Long vests and coats were lined with fur, or stuffed with cotton to ward off the chills. The cargo also included 476 piculs of lead.

Fair winds and a smooth passage brought the *Empress of China* swiftly across the Atlantic Ocean to the Cape Verde Islands, off the bulge of the continent of Africa. There the ship put in for supplies and fresh water. The crew acquired a pet, a little monkey with a black face. The next leg of the journey was southward to the Cape of Good Hope, thence north and east for the long passage through the Indian Ocean.

Five months out of New York, Captain Green sighted Java Head in the palm-fringed Straits of Sunda. As soon as the ship's anchor was dropped, scores of canoes, paddled by Malays, surrounded the *Empress of China* with boatloads of fresh fowl, fruit, turtles, and coconuts for sale to the sea-weary Americans. For half a dollar a fifty-pound turtle could be bought which would supply the ship's entire crew. A dozen fowl cost only one dollar. All the while from the terraced rice fields to the palm-lined shores came land breezes laden with the scents of new and strange spices.

Also anchored in the Sunda Straits at Java Head were two French ships, one of which was on the way to China, and the *Empress of China* was invited to sail along with her. The Americans accepted eagerly, happy to have company through the strange and dangerous waters ahead. The ships followed a route that would be increasingly well traveled during the next half century. They headed across the China Sea toward Macao, a port that had been under Portuguese supervision since 1557. The city of Macao was on an island, along the southern coast of the Chinese mainland, inside the mouth of the Pearl River, the only available gateway to Canton.

It was the season of the southwest monsoons, when favorable winds speeded ships along the China coast. The American ship and her French companion scudded before the prevailing winds to Macao, their last port before reaching Canton.

CHAPTER 4

A New Flag at Whampoa

AT MACAO a foreign ship received official permission to enter Chinese waters from a government officer, called a mandarin, who issued the permit, or "chop." Also at Macao arrangements were made to begin hiring skilled Chinese assistants, who were essential to the success of any trading voyage. The foreign merchants needed a linguist or interpreter to communicate with Chinese officials, merchants, tradesmen, and servants. It was forbidden for a foreigner to be taught the Chinese

Harbors at Macao: painting by unknown Chinese artist, about 1800

Ships at Bocca Tigris: painting by unknown Chinese artist, mid-nineteenth century

language, and most Chinese made no effort to become familiar with any foreign tongue. The linguist would also help arrange for riverboats and supplies for the foreign ship's officers and men.

Also vital to the journey was a Chinese pilot, usually a short man, of slight build, wearing his hair in a tradi-tional queue. The pilot, who would guide the ship up the Pearl River for the last eighty miles of the journey to Canton, came aboard at Macao, took his place behind the helmsman, and barked orders in short phrases of barely understandable English. With little sail, often no more than a foresail and a jib, the pilot directed the new ar-

rival slowly up the Pearl River through throngs of Chinese ships. Moving slowly past the *Empress of China*, heading downstream to the open sea, were great junks. Aboard the junks gongs often sounded; fireworks would explode; and pieces of red and silver paper were burned to be scattered over the waters as offerings to the ocean gods. The junks carried wands of powdered sandalwood, called joss sticks, which were ignited, giving off a sweet scent, to aid prayers for a fair wind. If the winds died down, the crew would toss overboard little boats made of gilt paper as offerings to break the calm.

Finally the *Empress of China* reached the Bogue forts, which guarded the mouth of the harbor at Canton. The forts were situated on the sides of a narrow gap in the rocks in the Pearl River, once known as the "tiger's mouth" or Bocca Tigris, from which they derived their name. Cannon in the Bogue forts were firmly anchored in the stone foundations and could not be swiveled or turned. As a result the guns could be fired in only one fixed direction, which made them somewhat dubious

Ship flying American flag: China trade porcelain, about 1790

Port of Canton with Dutch Folly Fort: China trade porcelain,
1750–1760

guardians for the city. Also protecting the port were round fortifications known as the Dutch Folly Fort and the French Folly Fort.

Beyond the Bogue forts was Whampoa, the anchorage for all foreign vessels in the Pearl River. At Whampoa ships of many nations, spread in a great arc, rode at anchor. Canton itself was another twelve miles up the river.

The journey from Macao to Whampoa took more than a day. As the ship neared the anchorage, the captain took over command of his vessel from the Chinese river pilot. Having selected his mooring, the captain inched slowly toward it, aware that his movements were being watched through telescopes from every bridge. The captain's skill as he maneuvered his ship to the anchorage was being closely observed.

On August 28, more than six months after she had set out from New York, the *Empress of China* eased her way into the crescent of ships at Whampoa, fired thirteen guns in salute, and dropped anchor. America had entered the China trade.

Foreign ship anchorage at Whampoa Reach: painting on glass, early nineteenth century

CHAPTER 5

Arrival at Canton

At Whampoa the *Empress of China* found
herself in the company of forty-five other vessels, each
flying the flag of a European nation. Immediately officers
from the European ships came aboard to greet the first
representatives of the new United States to reach China.
Even the British, forgetting the recent bitterness of the
Revolutionary War, proved to be warm and welcoming
in this distant part of the world.

To the Chinese, however, the Americans seemed a
curious contradiction. Here were people who spoke the
same language as the English, yet declared themselves
citizens of a different country. To distinguish them from
the English, the Chinese called the latest arrivals "New
People." The red, white, and blue Stars and Stripes, flap-

*Chinese vessels under sail: painting by unknown Chinese artist,
mid-nineteenth century*

Chinese ship and crew

ping in the ship's rigging, prompted the Chinese to name the new traders' country "the flowery flag kingdom."

The arrival of the *Empress of China* was immediately reported to the local authorities by the Chinese pilot, who gave the name not of the ship but of the captain. Two Chinese boats were then made fast to the anchored American ship to prevent any smuggling.

The chief Chinese customs inspector at Whampoa was known as the Hoppo. It was his responsibility to measure the incoming ship and to impose the only direct tax on the vessel and the cargo. This fee had to be paid into the treasury of the Chinese Emperor before any of the ship's cargo could be put ashore.

But before the Hoppo would determine the fee he had to be won over with "cumshaw"—gifts—for himself and his wife or mother, usually such things as watches, clocks, musical snuffboxes, or perfumes.

Once these preliminaries were satisfactorily completed, the ship's cargo could be unloaded into riverboats, known as "chop boats," and carried the twelve miles upstream to

Canton, where it would be taken ashore and stored in the spacious warehouses, called hongs. The hongs were also known as factories, from the word "factor," or agent. The last dozen miles between the Whampoa anchorage and Canton were not open to foreign shipping. In order to make arrangements with a hong merchant to unload the ship, Captain Green and the supercargo, Major Shaw, had to go up to Canton in one of the small, fast boats which plied the last few miles.

The Americans were swept through a world of sights and sounds utterly strange to them and were surrounded by Chinese vessels unlike anything they had ever seen. Some lined the riverbanks, while others floated downstream. There were great salt junks even larger than the *Empress of China*. Many vessels had huge eyes painted on their prows to watch for monsters and devils. Smaller craft were propelled by gangs of naked workmen, treading paddle wheels or pulling long oars. Gay, decorated flower boats floated by silently. And patrolling the area were the official mandarin boats, flying white and yellow

Chinese ship and crew

Boatmen on Chinese river craft: engraving, 1843

Scene on the Honan Canal, near Canton: engraving, 1843

Chinese commercial ship: engraving, 1845–1847

River scene, on fish platter and rack: China trade porcelain for American market, early nineteenth century

flags, with red sashes tied around the muzzles of their ships' cannon.

Nearing Canton, the riverboat carrying the Americans had to weave through a throng of tiny flat-bottomed sampans, narrow at the bow and stern but broad in the beam. Some of the sampans were carrying loads of cargo to and from the foreign ships at Whampoa. Others had elegant cabins, handsomely furnished, with ornamental bamboo roofs and shuttered windows. Along the banks of the river, thousands of houseboats were moored, each the home of a family, each with its small cooking stove in the stern, its decks cluttered with pots and pans. Baskets of fowl hung over the sides. Children played on the decks everywhere, a wooden buoy tied to their backs to keep them safely afloat if they fell into the water.

Captain Green and Major Shaw were soon near enough to see Canton's hong buildings. These structures were two or three stories high, set back about three hundred feet from the river. Flags of many nations flew over the sloping roofs. The Americans would soon be adding the Stars and Stripes to the display.

Sailing ship and pagoda: painting on paper, Chinese, nineteenth century

American and European flags flying over hongs at Canton: painting on glass, Chinese, early nineteenth century

Dignitary watching a scroll painter: painting on enamel dish, Chinese, eighteenth century

CHAPTER *6*

Hong Merchants in the Celestial Empire

FOR MANY YEARS there was only one way in which trade between the Western world and China could be carried on. The unique procedure, known as the Canton system, allowed Westerners to deal only with a single group of merchants, generally thirteen in number, known as the Cohong. The name Cohong was derived from Chinese words which meant "officially authorized guild." Each member of the group was known as a hong merchant. Some hong merchants accumulated great wealth in their dealings with the West; others failed, became impoverished, and even went to prison.

Even as late as the eighteenth century in China, merchants were held in low esteem by the Emperor and the ruling nobility. China, the oldest continuing civilization in the world, was still primarily an agricultural country, a feudal society of landowners and serfs. A few patricians owned vast estates; members of the landed classes became scholars and artists. The rest of the population were mostly land-working peasants, many of whom found themselves being driven off their farms by high taxes and crop failures. Merchants, or middlemen, of all nationalities were regarded with scorn.

Commerce and trade seemed of little importance in feudal China. The Chinese did not consider that they were in need of anything from the rest of the world. They believed that they already had the best possible food—rice; the best drink—tea; and the best textile—silk.

China called itself both the Celestial Kingdom and the Middle Kingdom, reflecting the belief that it was located in the very center of the universe over which it ruled. On the other hand, Europeans and Americans thought that they too were at the center of the globe, which is

Lady with attendant at river's edge: China trade porcelain made for Dutch market, eighteenth century

The Ch'ien-lung Emperor (1736–1795):
painting on silk, nineteenth century

why they referred to China as the Far East.

Recorded history in China goes back nearly four thousand years. During most of that time the Chinese were isolated from other great civilizations which grew up in the world, such as the Egyptian, Mesopotamian, Persian, Greek, and Roman. Throughout its long history China had been ruled by a succession of royal families, not all of them natives of the land. The last royal dynasty was the Ch'ing, which had held sway since 1644. The Ch'ing dynasty had been founded by a Manchu warrior chief who was called in to help drive out of the city of Peking a bandit enemy of the Ming emperor who was then ruling. Once the Manchu chief was successful, he saw no reason to give up the city he had taken.

The Ming dynasty, which was displaced by the Chi'ng, had ruled China for almost three centuries (A.D. 1368–1644). During that time some of the greatest masterpieces of Chinese art were created. Painters and poets flourished. The graceful porcelains known as Ming vases were produced.

It was during the Ming dynasty that the first western Europeans, the Portuguese, reached China. Christopher Columbus was looking for Cathay, as China was known to him, when he came on America. The discovery of the American continent was soon felt in Asia. From America came new plants—maize, sweet potatoes, peanuts, and tobacco—and new money, Spanish silver pesos.

Before the rule of the Ming, China had been under the foreign rule of the Mongols, among them the celebrated Kublai Khan. During this era, the Yüan dynasty, overland contact was established with Europe, as recorded by the traveler from Venice, Marco Polo.

When Captain Green and Major Shaw arrived in 1784, the ruler of China was the fourth emperor of the Ch'ing dynasty. He was known as the Ch'ien-lung Emperor, and he had occupied the Celestial Throne for almost fifty years. (The Ch'ing rule ended in 1911. The Republic of China was established in 1912, followed in 1949 by the People's Republic.)

The Ch'ien-lung Emperor expressed Imperial China's

Empress of Ch'ien-lung on dragon throne: painting on silk, nineteenth century

Mandarin in a sedan chair on a ceremonial visit: engraving, 1843

attitude toward merchants from the West in a letter to King George III of England: "Our dynasty's majestic virtue has penetrated unto every country under heaven, and kings of all nations have offered their costly tribute by land and sea . . . We possess all things. I . . . have no use for your country's manufactures. . . . You, O King, from afar have yearned after the blessings of our civilization. . . . But your . . . requests . . . completely fail to recognize the Throne's principle to . . . exercise a pacifying control over barbarian tribes, the world over. . . . My capital is the hub and center around which all quarters of the globe revolve."

The Chinese had little in common with the Europeans and Americans who came to Canton looking for teas and silks, while to the Westerners there was almost nothing about China that was familiar. As a result, little understanding developed between the ancient Empire and the commercial West.

When the *Empress of China* arrived, no official contacts had yet been established to help bridge the gap between the Imperial government of China and the nations of the Western world. There had been no exchange of diplomats and no official treaties. Gifts to the Emperor were viewed and accepted, not as compliments from friends and equals, but as tributes from subject rulers and people. Westerners were rarely permitted audiences with the Emperor and even then never as honored visitors. Approaches to the Emperor's throne involved an elaborate ceremonial procedure, which included the ritual of the kowtow. The ritual consisted of three occasions when the visitor knelt, and nine when he had to lie prostrate on the floor and bang his head. To the Chinese the kowtow was a mark of courtesy. The Emperor kowtowed to heaven; ministers performed the ritual before the king; common people prostrated themselves before government officials; children made the full obeisance before their parents. Refusal by the Westerners to perform the kowtow was regarded as insulting by the Chinese.

Dinner party at mandarin's home: engraving, 1843

Mandarin and family at home: engraving, 1843

High-ranking lady in her bedroom: engraving, 1843

Street scene in Canton: engraving, 1843

House of hong merchant near Canton: engraving, 1843

Westerners did not understand most Chinese attitudes, particularly the Chinese view regarding trade. Europeans considered that they had the right to carry on commerce and felt they could demand that the right be respected. The Chinese viewed trading as a special privilege, which was granted as a favor and could therefore be withdrawn. In the West trade was glorified; in China it was held in very low esteem.

The hong merchants in Canton were aware of the disdain with which the aristocrats of their own country regarded them. They knew they were constantly at the mercy of the Emperor or his officials. Even though the Chinese merchants had to pay a high price for the privilege of trading with the West, they could be called on at any time for additional sums. Whenever more money was demanded of the Chinese merchants, foreign traders found that the price of tea had gone up.

Every incoming ship from the West became the personal responsibility of a Canton merchant. He took charge of the merchandise brought in and arranged for the cargo for the return voyage. He was responsible for the conduct of every member of the foreign crew and he was subject to punishment when any of the crew misbehaved.

Best known of the hong merchants were Puankequa, Mouqua, and Houqua. (The suffix *qua*, at the end of the merchants' names, was derived from the Chinese symbol *kuan*, indicating an honorary title.) Each merchant usually wore a button that indicated his rank. The name of the hong merchant who arranged to handle the cargo of the *Empress of China* was Shynkinqua. In later years American trade in Canton would concentrate primarily around Houqua, whose real name was Wu Ping-chien. Several other members of the Wu family were also known as Houqua.

In spite of the official scorn in which the hong merchants were held, some of them managed to accumulate great wealth and to live private lives of almost royal splendor. On the rare occasions when foreigners were invited to a Chinese merchant's home, they were received

Houqua: painting, Chinnery school, nineteenth century

(43)

Fortuneteller outside his house: painting by unknown Chinese artist, about 1830

Kitchen quarters of a mandarin's house: painting, Chinese, mid-nineteenth century

Chinese garden scene, playing "go": painting by unknown
Chinese artist, mid-nineteenth century

in a many-roomed palace with marble floors, lavishly carpeted with velvets and silks. The rooms were usually filled with exquisite furniture, bronze statues, hanging scroll paintings, and displays of magnificent porcelain. Surrounding the house were carefully landscaped gardens, dotted with waterfalls that splashed gently into reflecting pools. Arched bamboo bridges spanned brooks in which swans swam gracefully. Peacocks promenaded through the grounds.

Guests were entertained elaborately. Meals often lasted for hours, with as many as thirty courses served in dishes as dainty as jewels. The wines were usually served in silver cups. Many Americans admired this Chinese life style and returned to the United States with a taste for Oriental manners and art.

Once the banquet was over, both the hong merchant and his foreign guests found themselves again under the cold, scornful eyes of Chinese officialdom. But the Americans, like the Europeans before them, learned to endure it in silence.

CHAPTER 7

Foreign Life in Canton

CAPTAIN GREEN AND Major Shaw stepped out of the riverboat that had sped them up from Whampoa, climbed a flight of stairs, and found themselves in an open court before the hong warehouses. They had finally reached their destination—a cramped area, squeezed between the Pearl River and the city's walls, where they would live and carry on their business for the next few months.

What greeted the first Americans to set foot in Canton was a bustle of excited activity. The streets around the hongs were filled with sailors of many nationalities, wandering from shop to shop along Hog Lane and Old China Street at either end of the foreign area. Connecting the

Hong buildings at Canton: painting by unknown Chinese artist,
1800–1815

streets and separating the hongs from the city walls was Thirteen Factory Street, which was also crowded. On sale in the shops were wide varieties of merchandise: fireworks, bird cages, medicines, ivories, silks, and even cats and dogs. For thirsty throats there was a fiery local wine called *samshu*, meaning "thrice fired."

All the excitement, however, was restricted to the tiny section of Canton that was open to visitors from the West. They were forbidden to leave the area assigned to them. They were not allowed to wander into the city itself or to take walks in the surrounding countryside. Many a China trader spent lonely hours pacing up and down before the hong buildings, impatiently waiting for the hour when he could rejoin his family.

Although it was often dreary, life in Canton could also be luxurious for the foreign visitor. The trader would have servants to care for every need. Meals were often sumptuous, delicately prepared, featuring dishes of sharks' fins, plovers' eggs, and octopus.

When at a later time restrictions were relaxed a little,

European man playing with parrot: painting on hanging silk scroll by unknown Chinese artist, eighteenth century

Street vendor selling cakes and fruits: watercolor by unknown Chinese artist, mid-nineteenth century

the rules were still confining: Foreigners were granted special leave to organize excursions across the river to visit the nearby flower gardens or taverns four times a month. But the official rules demanded that the visitors not go about in "droves" of more than ten persons at a time, and they were not allowed to row on the river for recreation.

Almost forty years after the Americans first reached Canton, a fire swept the waterfront and the appearance of the area changed. What had once been an open area reserved for the exclusive use of the foreign visitors was turned into a thoroughfare, in which local Chinese tradesmen would come to do business with the foreigners and local children would gawk at the strange behavior of the "barbarians." There would be Chinese tailors, jugglers, barbers, cobblers, and entertainers, with long stories to tell. Hawkers sold olives, lichee nuts, and Chinese pastry. Beggars stretched out hands for alms. On occasion the Chinese police would clear the square, beating off the beggars and peddlers with long whips. Most of the time the street was so congested that it was almost impossible to elbow one's way through.

But at nightfall the scene changed. The native Cantonese left the streets around the hongs and returned to their homes inside the city walls. The foreign area grew quiet, seemingly deserted.

Green and Shaw reached Canton at the end of summer, just as the busy months of buying and selling were about to start. The season would last through the autumn while favorable winds from the South hurried along more ships eager to trade for the piled-up crates of tea and porcelain and the colorful bolts of silk.

Winter brought a shift in the winds. The trading season ended and all Europeans were expected to leave Canton and return home or at least go back to Macao, where Westerners had been living for two centuries. The Chinese did not want even a suggestion of a permanent home for foreigners in Canton. For this reason one rule was iron-clad: "Neither women, guns, spears, nor arms of any kind can be brought to the factories." One American

Acrobat dancing on a tightrope: watercolor by unknown Chinese artist, mid-nineteenth century

*Entrance to a mandarin's house; procession with sedan chair: painting
by unknown Chinese artist, mid-nineteenth century*

*Forecourt of a mandarin's house: painting by unknown Chinese artist,
mid-nineteenth century*

The Great Temple, Macao: engraving, 1843

girl, Harriet Low, tried to elude the ban by slipping into the city dressed as a man, but she was immediately discovered and sent back to Macao.

In the winter the men came down to Macao from Canton to stay with their wives and families. Their lives were leisurely; they kept many servants and enjoyed numerous diversions, such as horse racing, cricket matches, and tea parties. The picturesque city of Macao was set in the midst of terraced hills. Some of the homes of the China traders looked out over the straits, commanding a view of the Pearl River.

As soon as the new season's teas began to reach Canton, the men left their homes in Macao to return to the lonely hongs. In Canton the whitewashed buildings of the hong merchants stood back a few hundred feet from the river. Inside the hongs were storage areas, called "godowns," for chests of tea and bales of silk that had been piling up in anticipation of the arrival of the foreign ships. In the upper stories were living quarters which were rented to visiting ship captains and supercargoes.

Some of the hongs had wide verandas, supported by grand pillars; many of the buildings were connected.

The hongs were the domain of the Chinese merchants. Here the foreign traders came to find out what prices the Chinese had set on their cargoes. Prices on all articles fluctuated, for many reasons. For example, the price of imports would drop if too many ships were in the harbor at any one time, creating an oversupply. Chinese tea would cost more if the crop proved meager. New taxes or a sudden demand for more money from the Emperor's court would result in higher prices. The fluctuation in the prices of the trade goods could spell fortune or disaster for the overseas trader.

Each hong merchant employed a staff skilled in the complexities of the trade. The agent for the Chinese merchant was known as a *Fiador*. Acting as cashiers and accountants were *Compradors*, who also served as purchasing agents to arrange provisions for the foreign ships. *Schroffs*, or silver masters, weighed and tested the gold or silver which the traders often used as currency in buy-

Hongs in Canton: China trade porcelain,
late eighteenth century

ing Chinese goods. If any other currency was tendered, the Schroffs evaluated it. Scribes and clerks kept the voluminous accounts.

Linguists acted as go-betweens for the Chinese officials and the foreign visitors. Communication was difficult between the Chinese and the many Europeans who came to Canton, each speaking a different tongue. A common speech developed, consisting primarily of English words, with some additions from Portugal, India and China. Eventually this dialect became known as business or "pidgin English."

Many of the words have since become accepted in English usage, as "mandarin" from the Portuguese word *mandar*, to order. Other words derived from the Portuguese that were used in pidgin English were "Comprador" from *comprar*, to buy; "joss," from *deus*, meaning God; "la-le-on" from *ladrão*, a thief; "grand" from *grande*, the chief; and "junk," meaning a Chinese ship, from the Portuguese pronunciation of a Chinese noun. Words originating from India were "bazaar," a market; "Schroff," a money lender; "tiffin," luncheon; "godown," from *ka-dang*, a warehouse; "lac," meaning one hundred thousand; "coolie," a laborer; "chit," a note; "bungalow," a cottage.

CHAPTER 8

Americans in the Hongs

ONCE ASHORE IN Canton, Captain Green and Major Shaw made arrangements to dispose of the cargo

European merchants in a chinaware shop: China trade porcelain,
1725–1740

from America. The large shipment of ginseng, the furs, woolens, cotton, and lead were unloaded and stored in one of the ground-floor go-downs, which for the next four months resounded with voices of buyers and sellers. Meanwhile a cargo was being assembled for the long voyage home. Two varieties of tea, black and green, were put on board. There was almost five times (2460 piculs) more black tea than green (562 piculs). Added to the cargo were pieces of handwoven cloth, called nankeens, after the city of Nanking, where the cotton fabric had originally been manufactured. Almost a thousand piculs of chinaware were stowed along the bottom of the hull. The remainder of the shipment consisted of 490 pieces of silk and 21 piculs of cassia, or Chinese cinnamon.

The Americans were eager to buy as much tea as possible. An opportunity arose to increase their purchases with the arrival of another ship, the *Pallas*, a former India trader, Captain John O'Donnell in command. Thomas Randall, the assistant supercargo, chartered

River craft in front of hongs: engraving, 1843

O'Donnell's ship and followed the *Empress of China* with an additional cargo of chinaware and tea.

CHAPTER *9*

The Brew of the Immortals

To the Western world tea was China's most desirable and valuable export. Since the beverage had been introduced into England and her possessions in the middle of the seventeenth century, its popularity had increased rapidly. The demand for elegant porcelain teapots and for sets of colorful cups and saucers also grew steadily.

In China the stimulating drink had been known for centuries. The word "tea" itself was of Chinese origin. The earliest cultivation of the tea-growing shrubs probably began hundreds of years ago in the interior of China; from there it expanded gradually down the river valleys until it reached the coast.

Tea was grown wherever there was a spare plot of land. Every patch along the hillsides, near the bends in the rivers, or surrounding the rice fields was planted. The tea growers were usually small farmers, working their own family gardens. They tended to their precious tea bushes with great care, sheltering them from the cold monsoon winds that blew during the winter months. The tea shrubs were planted and transplanted, weeded, pruned, and clipped. In three years the first flush of tea leaves could be picked. It took from four to seven years longer for the bush to become full bearing. The life of a tea bush could be as long as fifty years. During this time the tea plants produced four flushes of new shoots each season. The flavor and quality of the tea leaf depended on the age of the shoot, the soil in which the shrubs were growing, and the season and weather in which the leaf was picked.

The tea trade, from planting to export: painting, Chinnery school, about 1835

Workmen in the tea trade: China trade porcelain, 1740–1750

All teas come from the same shrub, but different types of tea result from various methods of processing. Sometimes the freshly picked leaves were partly dried in the sun or set in heated trays for about a day. Then they were gently rolled for about three hours to press out the plant oils. Sometimes the tea leaves were dried again for thirty or forty minutes.

The main varieties of tea were black, green, and oolong. Black tea was allowed to mellow or ferment in baskets; sometimes the leaves were spread out on long glass shelves, for periods ranging from a half hour to four and a half hours. Green tea was steamed without being left to ferment. Oolong tea, meaning "black dragon," combining characteristics of both the fermented black types and the unfermented green varieties was allowed to ferment, or oxidize, but was checked halfway and dried. The different names given to Chinese tea indicated the area where the leaf was grown or the season in which it was picked. Many names became familiar in the United States: Bohea, a mispronunciation of the Wu-I hills; Congou, which signifies a "workman's brand"; and Souchong, meaning "small variety." There were other well-known types: Young Hyson, indicating that the tea had been picked "before the rains"; Hyson, signifying "vigorous spring"; Gunpowder, meaning "small pearls"; and Imperial, the name for "large pearls." The popular Pekoe, meaning "white hair," was named for the down which appears on the new tea leaf just as it is opening.

Early in the year tea merchants by the thousands came down from the interior hills to Canton to arrange for the delivery of the spring crop. At the same time the first American trading ship, the *Empress of China*, was on her way from New York. During the months that the ship was at sea, the warm spring rains watered the tea plants in the interior. New shoots would be budding, to be picked, dried, and packed for the long journey to the hongs at Canton.

Workmen packing tea: China trade porcelain, 1740–1750

After the tea had been picked and processed, its first destination was the nearby tea merchant. If the tea leaf was a choice pick, it would be carried in a cask by a bearer, who would carefully prevent it from touching the ground so that no mud or sand could get mixed with it. Lesser grades were handled less cautiously. They were carried in chests hanging from a pole on the bearer's shoulders.

Once assembled from the producing area, the tea crop was sent on to Canton. Overland routes, some longer than eight hundred miles, might require several months of travel. A journey down an inland waterway was speedier but more expensive, because the tea passed through impost stations where extra duties were levied. When the tea reached Canton, it was piled up in the merchants' warehouse, where it waited for the southwest monsoons to blow in the trading ships.

The choice green Hyson tea arrived in chests already cured. The black Bohea was delivered in baskets, partially cured, and then dried in the cool autumn air.

When a shipment of tea had been arranged for delivery to a foreign vessel, chests were set up along the floor of the factory and baskets of tea leaves were emptied into them. Workmen stepped into each of the chests and trod upon the leaves to crush them. The workmen were not allowed to wear shoes for fear the tea leaves would be bruised.

Dealings with the Chinese merchants were conducted by gentleman's agreement. There were often no written contracts, and few willful breaches of agreement took place. The hong merchants sold an entire cargo of tea from a few samples, called musters, taken at random from several canisters. The weight of the tea shipment was determined by taking an average of a few chests. The usual practice in buying tea was to set the price in advance. However, since the *Empress of China* was the first American ship to trade in Canton, her cargo of tea was probably paid for at current prices.

River scene: China trade porcelain, early nineteenth century

CHAPTER *10*

A Chinese Secret: Silk

SECOND ONLY TO its demand for tea was the West's eagerness for Chinese silk—the light and lustrous material that had been known in China for centuries.

For three thousand years sericulture—the cultivation of silk—had been a carefully kept secret. Only the Chinese knew how to nurture the precious eggs of the mulberry silkworm, how to feed the larvae and cherish the cocoon until the wriggling worms were transformed into moths. The Chinese cultivated the mulberry trees and prepared the leaves on which the silkworms fed. All stages of the silk-making process were carried on by Chinese women. They unwound the cocoons into continu-ous strands several hundred yards long, dyed the threads, and spun and wove them into shining cloth.

The secrets of silk breeding were guarded by imperial decrees. Disclosure meant death by torture for any informer.

The luxury of silk became known in the Western world as the result of Alexander the Great's military campaigns in Asia. To the ancient Greeks the Chinese were the "silk people." Later a caravan route, called the "silk road," stretched across the continent of Asia.

Throughout the centuries efforts were made to discover China's silk secrets. According to a legend, the eggs of the Chinese silkworm were smuggled out of the country by traveling monks, who hid the precious larvae in the hollows of their canes. Another story tells of a Chinese princess, on the way to her wedding to a foreign prince, who could not bear to be without her favorite material, so she hid silkworm eggs in her towering headdress.

Silk had been vital to the economic life of China since

Silk cultivation—collecting mulberry leaves: album leaf painting on paper by unknown Chinese artist, nineteenth century

Silk cultivation—tending the silkworms: album leaf painting on paper by unknown Chinese artist, nineteenth century

Silk cultivation—skeining the thread: album leaf painting on paper by unknown Chinese artist, nineteenth century

Silk cultivation—weaving cloth: album leaf painting on paper by unknown Chinese artist, nineteenth century

ancient times. Prayers were offered for success in breeding the worms and tending the mulberry trees. A Chinese empress set an example for the aristocratic women of the court by personally cultivating mulberry leaves, raising the worms, and reeling the silk fiber. For many years balls of silk thread were considered so valuable that people sometimes used them instead of money inside the country.

While the American colonies were still under British rule, several attempts were made to raise silkworms and to produce silk in the colonies of Pennsylvania and North Carolina. As late as 1830 efforts were still being made to promote sericulture in the United States. However, conditions in America proved to be unsuitable, and the projects failed.

Silk was always one of the most desirable of China's trade commodities. America's first traders were eager to bring back a sizable shipment of the precious cloth. Almost five hundred pieces of silk fabric were stowed on board the *Empress of China*.

CHAPTER *11*

Ships' Ballast

COLORFUL PORCELAIN DISHES, generally known as "chinaware" or simply "china," were eagerly sought in the markets of the Western world. Ship captains and seamen came home from the Far East with choice sets for their wives or sweethearts, which they hoped would make up for the long months of their absence. China trade porcelain included a wide assortment of plates, cups, saucers, bowls, and pitchers. Included were ornamental vases for the mantelpiece in the parlor or the sideboard in the dining room. Especially elegant were five-piece arrangements called garnitures, which were proudly displayed on the mantel. Large urns were prized as showpieces, marks of the status of their owners.

(70)

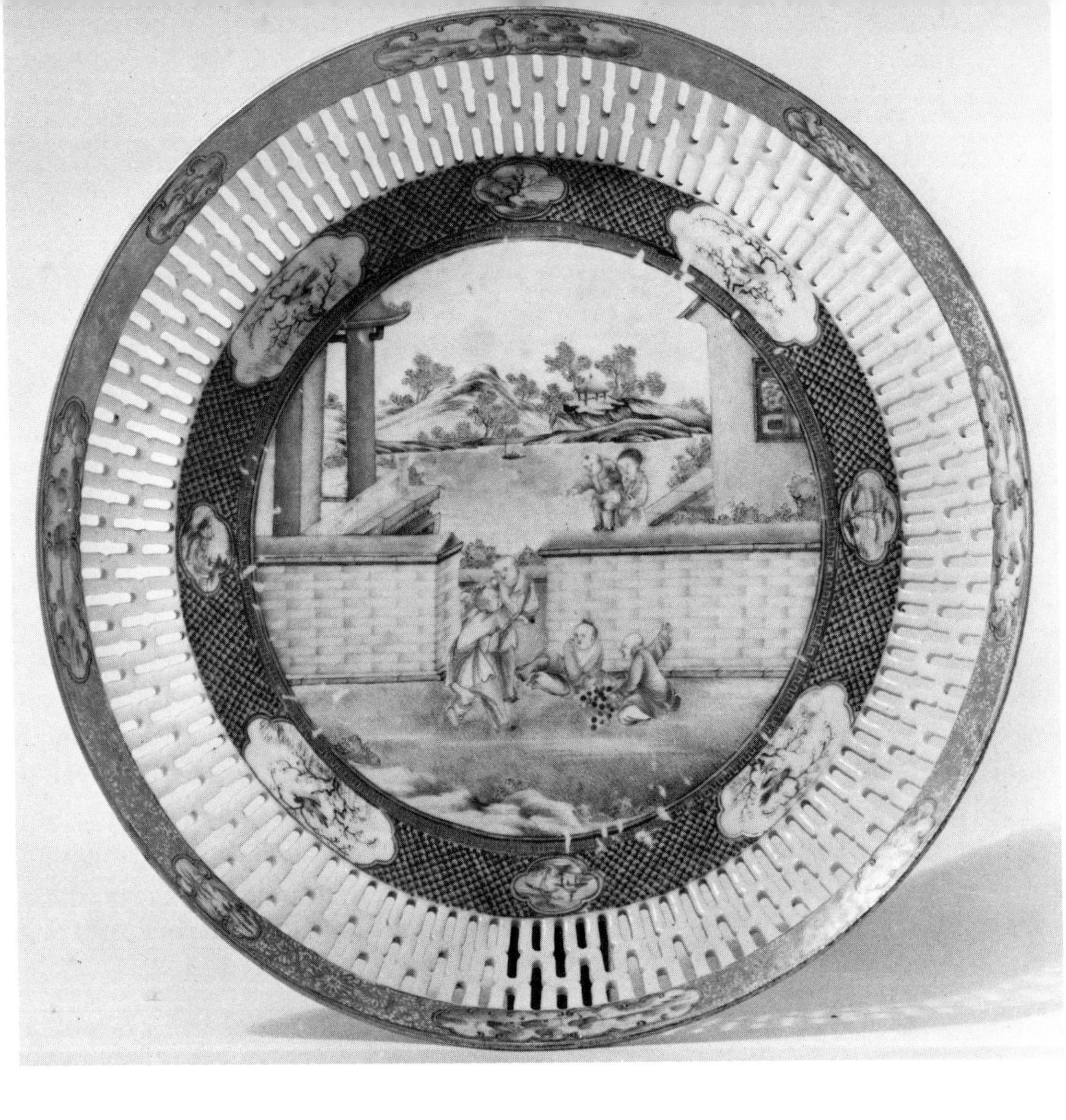

Chinese porcelain for the export market was commonly decorated with blue or rose designs on a luminous white background. Miniature landscapes with exotic temples and pagodas were popular.

At Canton, chinaware packed in crates and baskets was carefully stowed in the bottom of the ship's hold, where it served as a floor on which the main cargo of tea could be kept dry. The load of porcelain acted as a counterweight for the masts and sails overhead. The weight of the chinaware served as a ballast, holding the vessel steady at sea. For the return voyage to New York, sixty-four tons of porcelain were put aboard the *Empress of China*.

To the Chinese, porcelain is any fine-grained stoneware that is baked at extremely high temperatures and that rings when struck. Porcelain-like ceramics were first made in China about two thousand years ago, and the techniques were developed through the centuries. The translucent white porcelain which was highly admired in the West was being made as early as the T'ang dynasty (A.D. 618–906).

Chinese porcelain is made from two main ingredients. One is *kaolin*, a white clay that can be shaped and molded, named for the mountainous area Kao-ling, or "high ridge," in the province of Kiangsi. The second ingredient, *petuntse*, meaning "little white bricks," is a preparation containing feldspar, white clay, and silica. Combining the two ingredients is necessary to make porcelain; the *kaolin* will hold its shape when formed by the potter, but the *petuntse* is essential because it melts during the firing process and permeates the mixture. The varying proportions of the two ingredients determine the quality of the porcelain being made.

When the clay mixture has been properly prepared, the potter takes a bit of it, called a loaf, and throws it in the center of a revolving wheel. Craftsmen worked on an assembly-line basis, with as many as seventy persons engaged in the production of chinaware for export. Each potter made cup after cup, handle after handle, bowl after bowl. Each worker was a specialist in one step of the process or one form of the pottery. Sometimes, to fill the vast orders from overseas, the porcelain maker

Dish with openwork, decorated with scenes of children playing, birds, flowers, and landscapes: China trade porcelain, eighteenth century

Porcelain production, digging for kaolin and petuntse: water-color on paper by unknown Chinese artist, 1800–1810

Buffalo breaking up the large lumps

Carrying it to the warehouse

Mixing raw clay with water

Spreading it in the sun to dry

Beating it and bringing more water to mix with it

Transporting the clay in boats

Using the potter's wheel

Shaping the clay

Forming bowls

Laying them out to dry

Decorating the clay objects

forced the clay loaf over a mold, which was spinning rapidly on his potter's wheel.

Decorating the porcelain was also an art. Underglaze patterns were painted on with great care and skill. A mixture of cobalt oxide was used to produce a rich blue color. Glaze, made from a mixture of *petuntse* and water, was applied to the vessel, either by dipping or brushing. Once the glaze had dried, the pieces were placed in cases of clay, called saggers, to protect them, then stacked in a kiln.

The kilns were domed chambers made of clay bricks. They were usually twenty feet high, ten feet wide, and thirty feet long. Packed with firewood, the kilns were closed except for an opening sufficient to let in enough air to keep the fires burning. The firing process usually lasted for several days, during which temperatures inside the kiln went up to nearly 3000 degrees Fahrenheit.

Some porcelains came out of the kiln to be decorated with new designs and colors. Various mineral compounds, such as iron, copper, and manganese were used

Putting the objects in the kiln

Sealing the kiln door

Starting fires in the kiln

Removing the fired porcelain, packing and weighing

Painting the porcelain

for overglaze decorations. The pieces were fired a second time but at a much lower temperature. Overglaze decorating was done at the kilns; however sometimes, for special designs, it might be delayed and painted on at the seaport, before the pieces were packed aboard ship. Many patterns for export were standard, with each painter having his own specialty—a flower, a bird, or a pagoda—which he did over and over again.

Porcelain was made in many places all over southern and eastern China and still is today. But the main center of porcelain production was the town of Ching-te Chen, on the banks of the Ch'ang River, southwest of the Kaoling mountain area. Ching-te Chen was not a proud town like other Chinese communities. There was no wall encircling it. It was not the home of educated men, writers or scholars, who would lend it distinction. Since the beginning of the Ming dynasty early in the fifteenth century, when the Imperial Factory was established there, Ching-te Chen had been dedicated to a unique role: porcelain making.

Applying overglaze

Near Ching-te Chen were large supplies of all the materials necessary for making high-grade porcelain. The countryside surrounding the town contained hundreds, if not thousands, of kilns. Their fires filled the sky with clouds of smoke by day and painted it a perpetually glowing red by night.

Porcelain from China, some made as early as the tenth century, was exported to many islands in the Pacific Ocean and to the territories bordering the Indian Ocean from Indonesia to the Persian Gulf. Chinaware, equally old, has been found down along the east coast of Africa. Europe became aware of porcelain production in China from the accounts of Marco Polo, the thirteenth century Venetian. After Europeans reached China in the sixteenth and seventeenth centuries, porcelain in great quantities was carried back to England, Holland, Portugal, and other countries.

In Colonial America buyers of Canton china would have placed their orders with a merchant in London. When the War for Independence was over, an American

Refiring the porcelain

Packing the porcelain

Selling porcelain to Canton merchants

Loading boats for Canton

Celebrating with a play

*Transporting porcelain overland: from Ching-te Chen to Canton, painting
by unknown Chinese artist, late eighteenth century*

Packing porcelain in Canton for shipment to the West: watercolor by unknown Chinese artist, about 1830

could buy directly through a sea captain or China trader. Generally, he could choose from a pattern plate, which offered varied samples of porcelain decoration. His order would be filled in one of the many porcelain shops in Canton. Special orders, however, required individual handling. Chinese artists were extremely skillful at copying any pattern or device supplied to them. Some of the orders were for private coats-of-arms or patents of nobility, which many early Americans affected. One Chinese porcelain painter reproduced all the heraldry and armorial decorations with absolute fidelity, including even the instructions: "Copy these arms exactly," and "This is the drawing to copy."

Chinaware could be bought at Canton for comparatively little. A tea set of fifty pieces—cups, saucers, pitchers, and similar items—was priced at about three dollars. More elaborate settings, some numbering one hundred and seventy pieces, might command twenty-two dollars. The price would increase if the porcelain was decorated with a special design.

Signing of the American Declaration of Independence: Chinese porcelain vase, 1850–1900

"The Sailor's Farewell": China trade porcelain punch bowl, late eighteenth century

CHAPTER *12*

Life Aboard a China Trader

WHEN A CHINA trade vessel dropped anchor at Whampoa, the ship's crew could look forward to staying from two to three months. During that time ordinary seamen lived aboard the vessel, while the captain and supercargo went on to Canton and rented quarters in one of the hongs. The crew spent most of its time overhauling the ship for the homeward voyage, cleaning the hull, painting the decks, repairing the masts, the rigging, and the sails and generally putting everything into "shipshape" condition. For recreation the sailors from one ship would visit the crew of another. Or they could find entertainment in nearby Whampoa, where there were also curio and novelty shops. When they were granted leave, they usually went up to Canton.

Life aboard a sailing ship was far from easy. Captains and mates, many with experience on wartime privateers, became officers on commercial ships with little difficulty. However, ordinary seamen had to learn the fundamentals of seamanship, sometimes at the risk of their lives. The ship captain's rule was absolute. Officers' commands had to be followed without question, and obedience was often enforced with a heavy hand. Flogging a seaman was not uncommon.

Members of the crew came aboard with sea chests filled with their clothing and personal possessions. There was no uniform dress. Sailors were known to have bartered away warm clothing while they were in the tropics, only to regret the action once the ship reached the colder climates. Quarters for the crew were in the cramped forecastle, where the ordinary sailors slept in hammocks, sometimes drenched with seawater. Food was usually dried beef, which had to be washed down with a mixture of tea and coffee, called slops. Ship's news spread below decks primarily by rumors, exchanged around the barrel of drinking water known as the scuttlebutt. The crewmen were always delighted when the ship could put in at a port where stocks of fresh meat, fruits, and vegetables were available.

Work schedules at sea were rigid, with strict hours for keeping the watch and for resting. Often the wind and weather at sea would keep crewmen busy night and day, hoisting sails, lowering sheets, holding a course, tacking against the wind, running before a blow, or doggedly battling the waves that poured over the ship. In 1800 the ship *Hope,* from New Haven, tried for two months to sail around Cape Horn at the southern tip of South America, and had to give up the attempt. The following year the *Diana,* of New York, failed to complete the same passage after trying for a full month. Both ships finished their voyages by sailing around the Cape of Good Hope at the lower tip of Africa.

At other times the winds were favorable and the sea calm. When the monsoons were blowing from the right quarter, ships, their sails filled with the wind, scudded along, on their courses. Days went by without a change of sail. During those hours the younger seamen learned practical navigation from their more experienced shipmates. In turn the youngsters might teach their fellows to read and write. Many sailors kept journals of their travels, some of which were published. Samuel Shaw's journal of his experiences as supercargo of the *Empress of China* was widely read.

Seamen also brought home with them a wide variety of souvenirs, as well as porcelain, silk, and lacquerware, which could be sold for their own profit. Sometimes the souvenirs were ivory objects; sometimes even caged birds with brilliant plumage. Chinese clothing was a popular purchase, and the colorful garments were proudly displayed back home.

Hand-painted wallpaper: Chinese, early eighteenth century

*Miniature ivory pagoda, said to have been brought back by
Samuel Shaw, eighteenth century*

CHAPTER *13*

New York Takes the Lead

Besides assembling a cargo for his return voyage, Captain Green had a few private transactions to complete in Canton for the sponsors of the *Empress of China*. Robert Morris had commissioned the captain to buy some things for himself and his wife: four fans, some silk rolled on bamboo rods to be used as window shades, and some hanging decorations made of paper. He also received four small boxes of porcelain figures and a miniature stone pagoda.

A captain in the China trade enjoyed the additional privilege of being able to make private purchases on his own, which he could sell to add to his profit from the voyage. Captain Green's personal list consisted of umbrellas, some china bowls, extra yards of silk, tea, satin shoes, and one hundred and thirteen pairs of satin breeches.

In December 1784, ten months after she had departed from New York, the *Empress of China* received the "Chow Chow Chop"—the final clearance to leave Canton—and began her homeward voyage. The monsoon winds had changed, now favoring the journey back.

On May 11, 1785, after a brief stopover at the Cape of Good Hope, the *Empress of China* reached New York. She dropped anchor in the East River and saluted the city with thirteen guns, as she had on her departure fifteen months earlier. A few days later the first goods ever to come directly from Canton in an American vessel went on sale in New York. The total profit of the voyage amounted to $30,727—a gain of 25 per cent on the original investment.

The successful voyage of the *Empress of China* inspired visions of far-off adventure and handsome profits in the imaginations of Yankees, young and old. In cities up and down the Atlantic coast, newspapers published glowing accounts of the ship's accomplishment. In every village on every waterway big enough to harbor a five-man sloop, people began to dream about the Far East.

A group of merchants gathered in a New York coffeehouse for a friendly discussion of the voyage of the *Empress of China* and decided to sponsor their own venture. Among the merchants was a Vanderbilt, a name well known in the commercial history of America. Their ship, the second to sail to Canton from New York, was the 84-ton sloop *Experiment*, less than one-fourth as large as the *Empress of China*. The *Experiment* was originally built as a riverboat for passenger service up and down the Hudson between New York and Albany.

Into the hold went a cargo primarily of ginseng root, packed in fifty boxes and fifteen casks, valued at $18,750. Also loaded on the ship were wine and other assorted merchandise, such as tar and turpentine, which were useful ship's supplies, tobacco leaf, snuff, and seventy-five dollars' worth of furs. The miscellaneous furs—black

Tontine Coffee House (building at left) New York, where registries were kept of all ships arriving and departing: painting by Francis Guy, 1796

and red squirrel, mink, red and gray fox, wildcat, bear, raccoon, muskrat, and spotted fawn—were intended to sample the market at Canton to find out whether any of them would appeal to a Chinese buyer. The ship also carried eighteen boxes of Spanish silver dollars, valued at $20,000. These Spanish dollars, minted in Mexico and South America, were the most acceptable currency in China. For protection against pirates, six cannon were stowed on board, and rifles and pistols were provided for the crew.

Captain of the *Experiment* was a former privateer, Stewart Dean, who was also a shareholder in the enterprise. Dean found the ship overflowing with so much cargo that he had to share his cabin with some of the freight. In return for the inconvenience he was allowed an increase in his private dealings for Chinese goods in the amount of $500. The crew of the *Experiment* consisted of six men and two boys.

Dean was not the only ship's master in New York harbor getting ready to set sail for China. While his rivals were waiting for the most favorable winds for the start of the journey, which usually came up in February, Dean's sloop sailed away on a gray day in mid-December.

When the *Experiment* finally reached Canton, the Chinese could hardly believe that she had made the long journey alone. They thought the ship must be a tender for a larger vessel.

Almost exactly a year after leaving New York, on December 19, 1786, the *Experiment* began her return voyage. Four months and twelve days later the sloop was back in the port from which she had started, with 600 chests of Hyson tea, 100 chests of Souchong, 3000 cotton nankeens, 26 chests of teacups and saucers, and 5 sets of breakfast china, all of which were sold at the considerable profit of $26,322, or 40 per cent of the original cost.

In the meanwhile the *Empress of China* had sailed to Canton again. On the second voyage Samuel Shaw did not go as the supercargo. Instead he remained in the United States as First Secretary of the War Department, serving with his former commander, General Knox, who had been named Secretary of War by President George Washington.

When the third New York ship, *Hope*, sailed for China, Shaw was back as supercargo. Captain of the *Hope* was James Magee, a former man-of-war commander during the American Revolution. Shaw was not only super-cargo—he was also the first American consul, a diplomatic role without pay or privilege. The rank of consul was valuable to Shaw in his dealings with Europeans in Canton, but the official status carried little weight with the Chinese authorities because China acknowledged no diplomatic ties with any Western country.

Soon after the first New York ships to Canton had returned, the pace of maritime life in the American states began to quicken. By 1787 more and more ships were heading out to sea. Trade with the West Indies resumed little by little, even though at first it had to be detoured through a Canadian port in order to evade the British ban. Virginia tobacco was on its way back to markets in London, and cotton and rice were being exported from the South, mainly the Carolinas and Georgia.

What American merchant seamen needed—a central government that would support the infant foreign commerce—was coming into being. In April 1789 the first Congress met under the new Federal constitution and immediately acted to protect the nation's merchant marine. That same year exports to England from Philadelphia increased to a point exceeding the prewar volume.

In time commercial pressure on the United States eased even further. Early in 1793 England and France went to war against each other, and both sides soon found themselves in urgent need of food and supplies. Since the United States remained neutral, the Americans could carry on trade with both countries. The British opened all their ports, including the West Indies, and the French also allowed American ships into her harbors. By 1805 New York could feel the commercial pulse in her port beating faster, as the larger mercantile houses expanded their business.

Yet it was difficult for the merchants in New York to know what trade goods could be sold profitably to the Chinese. Apparently the early cargoes of ginseng had oversupplied the market in Canton. With the price of the root dropping, there seemed no point in sending any more. New York's chief article of export then was grain, but there was no market for flour in China, where everyone ate rice. At the same time, Spanish silver, which was being used to pay for American goods, was being regulated by the United States government and only limited amounts were available for trade.

As the war between England and France continued, American shipping found itself in new difficulties. In order to prevent supplies from reaching the enemy, both England and France attacked neutral America. Soon the British navy began forcing American seamen to serve on British ships.

In December 1807 President Thomas Jefferson, trying to avoid open warfare with England, imposed an embargo on all American ships, ordering them to remain in port. He hoped to prevent a direct conflict on the sea.

One New York trader, John Jacob Astor, who had already made a fortune dealing with furs from the Great Lakes, worked out a plan to keep up trade contact with China. He petitioned President Jefferson to authorize a journey to Canton, the purpose of which was to take home a distinguished Chinese visitor. Permission was granted and Astor sent out his ship, the *Beaver*, early in 1808, while his competitors, forced by the embargo to remain at anchor, complained bitterly. Astor's rivals claimed that the Chinese passenger was not an important visitor at all, but only a petty merchant in disguise, or perhaps just a member of the ship's crew.

On the way to China the *Beaver* was ordered to cruise along the Northwest Coast, where, incidentally, a few thousand dollars' worth of furs might be picked up. A year later the *Beaver* was back from China, her hold filled with a variety of goods, which brought a profit of $200,000. During all that time all rival ships had remained tied up in port.

Attack on the Tonquin *by Northwest Coast Indians*

Astor proved to be less fortunate in later experiences with fur trading in the Northwest. One of his ships, the *Tonquin*, was overrun and destroyed. A trading post, which he named Astoria, the first settlement by Americans in the area, was taken over by the British during the War of 1812. Astor's activities, however, became extremely important in helping to establish America's claims to the vast northwest territories, now the states of Oregon and Washington.

By the time the War of 1812 was over, commerce with China amounted to about one-third of all of America's overseas trade. New York, at first a less active seaport than Philadelphia or Boston, had grown equal in importance, and as the volume of trade increased, New York took the lead.

New York harbor is deep and well shielded from ocean storms. It can be approached either from the open Atlantic Ocean or through the sheltered waters of Long Island Sound. The Hudson River flows into the sea at New York, providing additional anchorage for ocean-going vessels.

New York's commercial leadership was further advanced by the development of steam navigation, inaugurated in 1807 by Robert Fulton on the Hudson River. In 1815 steamboat service to Connecticut was begun on Long Island Sound. New York attracted additional passenger and freight traffic with the launching in 1818 of the first scheduled ocean liner service to Europe. And when the Erie Canal was opened in 1826, linking New York through the Hudson River to the Great Lakes and the West, even more commerce passed through New York harbor.

The year 1826 also witnessed the financial failure of Thomas H. Smith, who had carried on most of New York's trade with Canton during the early 1820s. Smith took reckless risks and imported so much tea that the market became hopelessly glutted. When the price dropped sharply, Smith was forced into bankruptcy. After a while the China trade picked up through the activities of two brothers from Connecticut, George and Nathaniel Griswold, who sent a fleet to Canton, where their blue-and-white checkered flags became

New York harbor: engraving by John Hill, about 1834

View of South Street from Maiden Lane: ink and watercolor by William James Bennett, 1828

familiar sights. Another firm, founded by Daniel Washington Cincinnatus Olyphant, supported so many missionary expeditions to the Orient that it became known as "Zion's Corner."

Later firms, Howland and Aspinwall, and in the 1840s the Low family—Seth, Abiel A., and William H.—established themselves as importers of Chinese products. Both employed captains who won fame in tall-masted ships. One was Robert W. Waterman, perhaps the hardest-driving captain from New York; another, Nathaniel B. Palmer, started with seal-hunting expeditions from Connecticut.

New York was well suited to handle its role as the leader in the China trade. By 1830 more and more ships from other Atlantic ports came back from China and put into New York to sell their cargoes. The city became the receiving port for most of the trade between the Atlantic seaboard and China.

CHAPTER *14*

The First Millionaire in America

SALEM HARBOR, IN Massachusetts just fifteen miles northeast of Boston, was not ideal. It was deep enough for the small fishing boats which used it before the Revolutionary War, and it provided a shelter for privateers during the war. But the harbor had a tendency to fill up with silt, which made it too shallow for a large sailing ship.

During the War for Independence speed at sea became essential if a ship was to avoid capture. Speed was equally important for the ships that became privateering sea raiders. The privateers created a new brand of American

Salem harbor as it looked in 1800: woodcut about 1880

seamanship, confident and daring. A Salem privateer, Captain Jonathan Haraden, fought numerous battles with the British at sea. One of Haraden's ships, the *General Pickering*, beat off an enemy vessel three times her size and much more heavily armed. All during the war men and boys from Salem went to sea on privateers, hoping to find both adventure and fortune. Some were not so lucky; their ships and savings were lost. Many never returned at all.

Then for a few years after the end of the Revolutionary War Salem was desolate and depressed. Much of its prewar prosperity had been founded on trade with the British West Indies, but with the peace Britain closed the West Indian ports to Salem's shipping. Among the ships that rode silently at anchor, waiting for some new opportunity, were two swift former privateers, the *Astrea* and the *Grand Turk*.

To revive the port's prosperity, a Salem shipowner, Elias Hasket Derby, scoured New England homes, barns, and warehouses for goods that he could trade or

Elias Hasket Derby: Frothingham portrait

sell somewhere in the world. Derby himself never went to sea but he sent his ships in every direction, looking for new markets. A Derby bark, the *Light Horse*, became in 1784 the first American vessel to enter the Baltic Sea to establish trading relations with the Russians. Soon afterward Derby's *Grand Turk*, was reconverted and sent off around the Cape of Good Hope to China.

The *Grand Turk* carried a cargo that resembled the grab bag of a Yankee peddler. There were homemade and home-packed hams, kegs of pork and beef, boxes of prunes, chocolates, and a few barrels of flour. There were also sugar, rum, and brandy, as well as iron bars, whale oil, tobacco, and assorted candles. The total value of the items has been estimated at $32,000.

For several months the ship meandered around Africa and the islands of the Pacific Ocean, putting in at one port after another. The motley items in the ship's cargo were sold; other supplies were purchased and turned over at the next port of call. The process was repeated four or five times.

On her next voyage from Salem, beginning in January 1786, the captain of the *Grand Turk* was Ebenezer West. At the Cape of Good Hope the ship crossed paths with the *Empress of China* bound for New York. When the *Grand Turk* finally reached Canton, she dropped anchor near the *Hope*, on which Samuel Shaw had made his second trip to China.

When the *Grand Turk* headed back to Salem, her hold was filled with a cargo worth more than three times the value of her initial shipment. The tea, silk, and porcelain, which were unloaded on the Salem docks were valued at more than $100,000. The success of the voyage of the *Grand Turk* gave Salem a reason to celebrate, and the governor of Massachusetts, John Hancock, drove down to the dockside to lend an air of ceremony to the opening sale.

The successful voyage revived Salem's spirits. Now there was a new supply of Hyson tea. Elegant Salem women dressed in garments of Chinese silk and gathered around tables grandly set with colorful chinaware.

Square-rigged ship, similar to the Grand Turk: *China trade porcelain punch bowl for John Lamb, first customs collector for the Port of New York, late eighteenth century*

Derby sent a number of small ships in search of merchandise, which was brought back to Salem and piled high in his warehouses and on his docks. The harbor was filled with the aroma of nutmeg, cloves, coffee, palm oil, wool, leather, and tobacco.

Soon Derby's *Astrea* was ready for the long voyage to Canton. Again the cargo was a hodgepodge of Massachusetts thrift, ingenuity, and hope. Also on board was a collection of goods assembled from ports in Europe and along the Atlantic coast of the United States.

The major item in the cargo of the *Astrea* was ginseng, collected from nearby forests. But there were also iron, "duck" cloth and hemp from eastern Europe, wine and lead from France, Spain, and Madeira, rum from the West Indies, and flour, tobacco, and other supplies from the cities of New York, Philadelphia, and Richmond, Virginia.

Many citizens of Salem were envious of Derby's gains and wanted a share of the profits. Any Salemite with an item to spare sent it along on the *Astrea* in the hopes of reaping a handsome return. This miscellany included 336 barrels of flour, 50 boxes of chocolate, 598 firkins (33,488 pounds) of butter, and 45 barrels of beef, as well as 345 boxes of whale-oil candles and 50 barrels of salmon, plus some silver. The ship's owner was paid a freight charge for the shipments, and the supercargo was entrusted with the task of getting the best terms possible in some Far Eastern port. The proceeds were reinvested in tea or silk or a set of china cups and saucers, which could then be resold in Salem. One Salem household sent along two boxes of ladies' shoes; another shipped nineteen dozen handkerchiefs; still others gambled with leather saddlery and harnesses.

On the captain's bridge of the *Astrea* as she headed out to sea was James Magee, the skipper who had recently brought the *Hope* back to New York. Captain Magee's young brother-in-law, Thomas Handasyd Perkins, was his supercargo. Perkins was destined to become one of Boston's most influential merchant princes.

Captain Magee set his course toward the Pacific Ocean

and the island ports, where food and supplies were awaited eagerly. Along the way the supercargo arranged to sell items from the ship's hold. Many of the homespun New England products were snatched up as though from the shelf of a country store. Even before the ship reached Canton, cargo for the homeward voyage was being put aboard: sugar, coffee, and such spices as nutmeg and pepper. The pepper was packed away in the farthest corners of the hull so that none could get mixed in with the chests of tea that would be put on board in Canton.

The *Astrea* reached Canton to find the port already filled with fifteen American ships, three of them out of Salem, owned by Derby himself. The surplus of New England goods forced prices to drop sharply. American ginseng was being sold at half the price it had originally commanded, and the cargo of the *Astrea* could be disposed of only at a loss. Two of Derby's ships had to be sold to provide cash to buy cargoes for the remaining

Elias Hasket Derby monogram on China trade porcelain: about 1795

two. One of the ships sold was the *Three Sisters*. Her supercargo was a young man from Salem named Nathaniel Silsbee.

In spite of these difficulties the *Astrea* returned to Salem with enough tea, silk, and chinaware to earn a handsome profit. Captain Magee and young Perkins had traded on their own account and had brought in additional chests of tea, porcelain, and silk, as well as hand-woven nankeens. As part of their trading privilege the captain and supercargo also imported floor mats, window frames, lacquerware, ivory boxes, paper hangings, sugar candy, ribbons, and other assorted items.

Derby, the owner of the *Astrea*, had asked for a few curios for himself: some ginger and a few china figures and flower pots. He also received a set of dinnerware, consisting of 171 pieces, and a tea service of 101 items, marked with his initials. Because of the success of his trading, he became known as "King" Derby. He was reputed to be America's first millionaire.

CHAPTER *15*

Captains from Salem

THE HOMEWARD-BOUND VOYAGE of the *Astrea* from Canton to Salem dragged on slowly for all hands. Young Nathaniel Silsbee, who had been without an official berth since the *Three Sisters* had been sold, took advantage of the long hours of the homeward voyage to study navigation. He wanted to become a sea captain.

Silsbee's experience aboard the *Three Sisters* had been something of a disappointment for him. To supplement his wages of five dollars per month, he had attempted a private "adventure" together with his father, a sea captain. The two Silsbees had pooled eighteen dollars, which they invested in six boxes of codfish to be sold in the Chinese market. The small investment had not proved successful because most of the fish spoiled on the outward passage.

On the return trip Silsbee learned his lessons in navigation well. When he finally reached Salem, he was able to join his father on sea voyages up and down the Atlantic coast. He was quickly named second mate and soon offered command of a sloop, in which he set off for the West Indies.

Silsbee's voyage turned out to be a perilous one. Furious gales lashed the ship, sending towering waves over her. On several occasions the vessel seemed about to sink. When Silsbee finally reached the West Indies, he was told his sloop was really unfit to go to sea, but the young captain refused to abandon his craft. He repaired the vessel as well as he could and sailed back, finally managing to reach Salem. In his home port the verdict was confirmed: The ship was definitely unseaworthy.

At nineteen Nathaniel Silsbee became the captain of a Salem ship, the *Benjamin*, 161 tons. His mate was twenty years old. With one exception the rest of the crew were all under twenty-one years of age. Silsbee had on board the *Benjamin* a mixed cargo consisting of Madeira wine, glass, saddles, hops, and tobacco, which he disposed of in the French island colony of Mauritius, off the coast of West Africa.

Silsbee's success, as a trader and as a sea captain, continued. One day he would become a leading figure both of his city and state, and be elected to the United States Senate.

Nathaniel Silsbee had two younger brothers, Zachariah and William, who also went to sea and became captains before they were twenty years old.

———————•———————

In 1797 a second Salem ship named *Astrea* was en route to the Philippine Islands with young Nathaniel Bowditch aboard as supercargo. Bowditch, the son of a sea captain, was originally apprenticed to a ship chandler, or supplier. Young Nathaniel had an extraordinary talent for mathematics and when he was not occupied with his duties as supercargo, he spent his time making observa-

tions of the stars, the sea currents, and any other navigational guides. He became expert at using the primitive navigation instruments then available—a sextant, a few erroneous maps, and Guthrie's Geographical Grammar. There were no accurate charts and no chronometers; ships sailed by dead reckoning—the direct observation of the stars.

As the result of his careful observations, Bowditch caught eight thousand errors in the tables of the books of navigation then being used. He prepared corrections, and then, deciding to write his own work on seamanship, he embarked on two additional voyages in order to add to his notations. In 1801 the first edition of his *Practical Navigator* appeared. The work was quickly translated into a dozen languages and became a standard treatise on ocean navigation.

Two years after his book was published, Bowditch was at sea again, captain of the ship *Putnam*, his destination Sumatra, for pepper. Almost home again on Christmas Eve, 1803, Bowditch was making his approach to

Mariner with telescope, ship chandler's sign: painted wood sculpture by unknown American, early nineteenth century

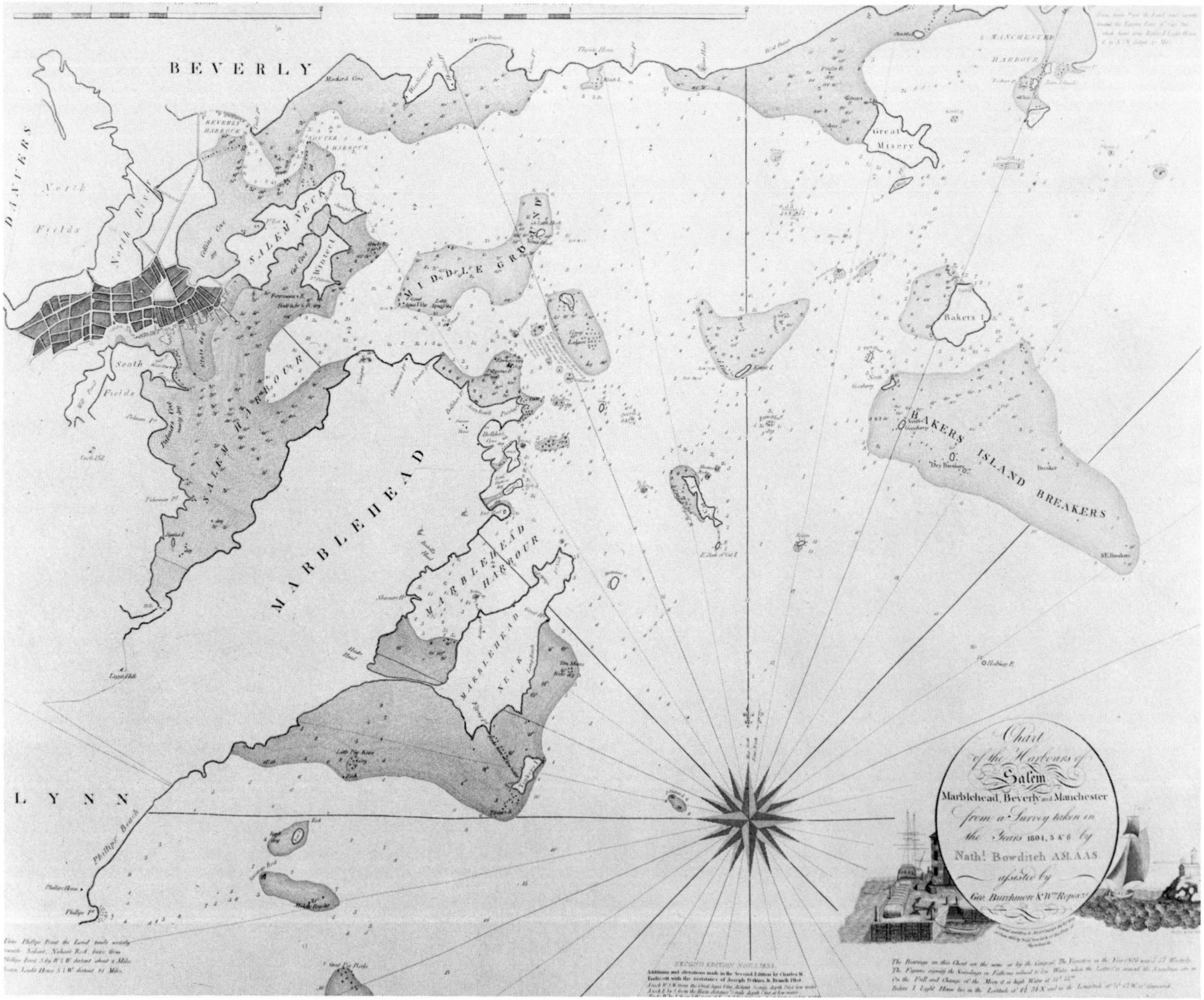
BEVERLY
DANVERS
North Fields
North River
SALEM NECK
Winter I.
BEVERLY HARBOUR
MIDDLE GROUND
Great Misery
MANCHESTER HARBOUR
Bakers I.
BAKERS ISLAND BREAKERS
South Fields
SALEM HARBOUR
MARBLEHEAD
MARBLEHEAD HARBOUR
MARBLEHEAD NECK
LYNN
Phillips Beach
Chart of the Harbours of Salem Marblehead, Beverly and Manchester from a Survey taken in the Years 1804, 5 & 6 by Nath! Bowditch A.M. A.A.S. assisted by Geo. Burchmore & Wm. Roper

Salem harbor in a blinding northeast snowstorm. Not a single landmark was visible to guide the navigating officer. But Bowditch's navigational charts were exact, and he picked the port out of the storm and entered the harbor without a mishap. Bowditch's reputation as a navigator was so widespread that any Salem man who could say he had sailed with the captain was assured of an officer's berth.

———•••———

Salem ships roamed the Pacific Ocean, trading with many ports in addition to Canton. These ships exchanged cargoes with the British at the Cape of Good Hope and in India, with the French in the islands off Africa, and with the Dutch in Batavia.

Spices from the Orient had been used in Europe for centuries to keep fresh meat from spoiling. The spices preserved the food, sharpened its taste, and disguised any bad odor once it began to spoil.

The word that pepper plants grew wild in northern Sumatra reached the ears of a Salem captain, Jonathan Carnes, while he was in a Pacific island port in 1793.

Chart of Salem and other harbors by Nathaniel Bowditch, 1804–1806

When he returned to Salem, Carnes arranged with a local merchant to equip a fast schooner, the *Rajah*, in which to gather the spice. With a crew of ten, a hold filled with brandy, gin, iron, tobacco, and dried fish, and with four cannon for defense, he set off for the Pacific, being careful to let no one know his destination.

For the next eighteen months there was no word from Carnes or the ship. When the sails of the *Rajah* were finally sighted once more, nearing his home port, he was greeted with cheers and flying flags.

Carnes came home with a shipload of pepper, which was sold for seven times the original cost of the voyage. It was so profitable that every ship's captain tried to pry the secret of its source from Carnes, but he would not tell where his pepper supply could be found. For three additional voyages Carnes managed to sneak away from his rivals and to bring back loads of pepper to Salem, but finally his secret was discovered.

For many years vessels from Salem supplied most of America's demand for pepper.

———•———

Crowninshield's Wharf, Salem: painting by George Ropes, 1806

The rivalry to bring in pepper from the Pacific islands filled the Crowninshield family of Salem with excitement. George Crowninshield, his sons, and his nephew were all interested in the spice trade and eager to profit from it. In 1804 a well-armed ship, the *America*, owned by the Crowninshields, was about to set off on her maiden voyage. Captain of the *America* was George's nephew. He sailed under direct and blunt orders: Proceed to the island of Sumatra for a cargo of pepper; nowhere else, for no other cargo.

Obeying orders was a rule of the sea, but the captain of the *America* had a mind of his own. At the island of Mauritius he heard such glowing reports of the market in coffee at Mocha that he decided to disregard his instructions about pepper. He set sail for the Red Sea, where he took on a full cargo of coffee and, in addition, quantities of gum arabic, hides, goatskins, and senna, a medicinal plant.

During the many months that Captain Crowninshield was at sea, the price of pepper in the Salem market fell sharply. During the same period the price of coffee rose.

In June 1805 the *America* was sighted off Salem, and two younger Crowninshields, desperately anxious about the incoming cargo, raced out to meet the homebound ship. As the Salem owners approached the vessel, they caught a surprising scent in the air.

"Coffee?" asked one hopefully.

"Probably the pot on the galley stove," snorted the other.

"What's your cargo?" shouted Benjamin W. Crowninshield to his cousin on the captain's bridge.

"Pe-pe-per!" the captain replied gleefully.

"You lie! I smell coffee!" roared Benjamin W. through his speaking trumpet. Benjamin W. Crowninshield would become Secretary of the Navy in 1814, serving for four years under President Madison and President Monroe.

Kamehameha II: lithograph by John Hayter, 1824

In 1795 Jacob Crowninshield brought back from India a sight that startled America: a huge Bengal elephant, the first ever seen in the United States. The mammoth beast arrived in New York for exhibition and was sold there for $10,000. Jacob and George, the first Salem Crowninshields to become seamen and China traders, were trained by their fellow townsman, Elias Hasket Derby. The next generation of Crowninshields consisted of four brothers, each of whom became a captain of his own ship before he was old enough to vote. In 1816 one of the Crowninshield brothers, George, Jr., became the owner of the luxurious *Cleopatra's Barge*, probably the first private yacht in New England. Some years later King Kamehameha II of Hawaii was so intrigued that he bought the yacht for his own use.

CHAPTER  *16*

The Cleveland Family

Seagoing was a proud tradition for many Salem families. Among the best known were the Clevelands, father and three sons. Of all the Clevelands the most illustrious proved to be Richard, whose seamanship amazed even his own contemporaries.

Stephen Cleveland, the father, went to sea for the first time unwillingly. He was forced to serve aboard a British man-of-war, but during the American War for Independence his naval experience proved valuable in the service of his native Massachusetts. He not only helped fit out privateers to harass British shipping; he became a member of the crew of one of the fastest armed ships out of Salem, the *Pilgrim*, which captured about fifty British prizes. Stephen Cleveland became the captain of the brig *Despatch*, the first American government ship to reach France and to return with a cargo of guns and military supplies. Flying from her rigging was the first American flag to be seen in France.

Stephen's son, Richard Cleveland, was born in Salem in 1773. At fourteen, he went to work in the mercantile house of Elias Hasket Derby to learn the commercial side of American shipping. Like so many other Salemites he began to risk his savings in little "adventures."

In four years Richard Cleveland was off to sea, his first voyage as a clerk for Nathaniel Silsbee on the *Benjamin*. Before the ship had returned to Salem, the eighteen-year-old Cleveland had been promoted to second mate. In five more years Cleveland was captain of his own ship, the bark *Enterprise*, bound for the coffee port of Mocha at the mouth of the Red Sea. The ship had reached Le Havre, France, when it was suddenly ordered home to Salem by the owners. Young

Captain Cleveland, however, refused to return with her. He sent the vessel back with the mate in command.

Deciding to start out on his own, he bought on credit a cutter named *Caroline*, only 43 tons, no larger than a fair-sized sailing yacht. Taking over the helm of the small cutter, Cleveland set sail for China, on the other side of the globe. On the first leg of the voyage, along the coast of France, he ran into stormy seas, lashed by furious Atlantic gales. The tiny ship, battered and wind-tossed, was driven ashore and damaged. Cleveland grimly managed to repair the ship and head back to sea.

Despite an inexperienced crew and unfavorable winds, the *Caroline* sailed across the equator, down the coast of Africa, and, three months after leaving France, reached the Cape of Good Hope. There the captain of a British man-of-war sighted the small vessel, hardly bigger than a cockleshell, and refused to believe that the ship had sailed all the way from Europe. The British, who were at war with France at the time, suspected the cutter of being a French spying boat, carrying secret messages, but no French dispatches were discovered. To avoid complications with Cleveland, who insisted that he was the owner of the *Caroline*, the British bought the vessel from him. The sale price of $5000 gave him a profit on his first venture. But once again the young Salem seaman was without a ship. He booked passage to the Dutch East Indies, but, finding nothing to interest him there, he proceeded to Canton.

Richard Cleveland soon bought another vessel of his own, a 50-ton cutter, *Dragon*, hardly larger than his first. He rounded up a crew, a tough gang made up primarily of men who had escaped from service on British warships or East India merchant ships. Some of the crewmen created so much trouble that Cleveland had to put six of them ashore on an island.

Cleveland headed the *Dragon* eastward across the Pacific Ocean toward the Northwest Coast of what is now the United States. For more than fifty days he battled the sea, finally bringing his ship to the inlets and rivers where the sea otter abounded. The fur of the sea otter was highly prized in Canton.

The Northwest Coast Indians, who were experienced traders, at first were generally friendly to the visiting seamen. In time, however, some of the Indians came to feel that they had been cheated by irresponsible captains, and they were quick to take revenge whenever they could. If they had seen how few crew members Cleveland had, they might have attacked him. But the young captain was resourceful. He hung a screen of furs along the sides of his deck so that the small size of his crew could be kept secret.

For two months the young American put into every possible cove and inlet, trading with the Indians for the valuable sea-otter skins. The Northwest coastal areas were still uncharted, and the perils of shipwreck and Indian attack remained constant. At one point Cleveland's little ship ran aground on a sunken ledge and lay helpless. The cutter had to be beached and rolled over on her side before she could be repaired.

During his two months on the Northwest Coast Cleveland managed to fill the hold of his ship with pelts that were later to bring $60,000 in the market at Canton. He counted his share of the enterprise at $40,000, plus an additional $6000 when he sold the cutter.

But even with his trading done at Canton, Cleveland was not yet ready to return to Salem. His cutter sold, he took passage on a ship traveling to India, after which he continued to the island of Mauritius, then known as the Île de France. There he teamed up with William Shaler of Connecticut to buy seven thousand bags of coffee to be shipped to Denmark. The partners journeyed to Europe with their investment, and in the German port of Hamburg they bought a fast, roomy brig, the *Lelia Byrd*, 175 tons. The two young men were ready to set out for further adventures.

The pair flipped a coin to determine who would be the captain of the *Lelia Byrd* and who the supercargo. Shaler won the toss and took command. Cleveland assumed the duties of the supercargo. In Hamburg the two Americans, both still not yet thirty years of age, found a friend who was happy to join their adventures. He was the Polish nobleman, Count de Rousillon. The count had served in the American War for Independence as an aide to General Kosciusko.

Cleveland, Shaler, and de Rousillon sailed into the Pacific Ocean and touched at various Spanish ports along the western coast of South America. Several of the coastal cities in Chile had forts protecting their harbors; they greeted the American ship with cannon fire.

On their way to China to dispose of a cargo of sea-otter fur, the two New Englanders and their Polish friend sailed to the mid-Pacific Sandwich Islands. Aboard the *Lelia Byrd* there was a horse, the first ever to be seen in Hawaii. The steed proved to be a sensational sight

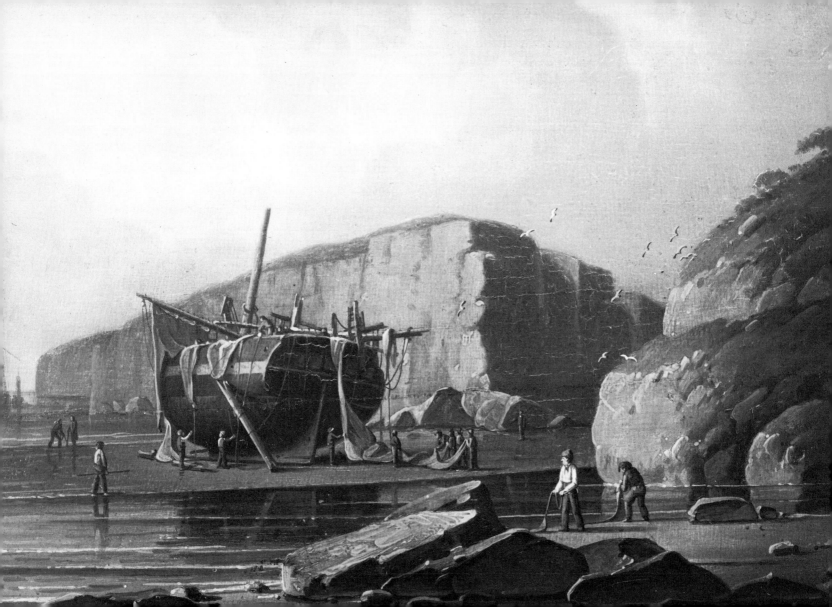

"*A View of Karakakooa in Owyhee (Oahu, Hawaii)*": engraving by
John Webber, 1778

"*Ship Aground*" by Robert Salmon, 1827

for the islanders, but their king, Tamaamaah—also known as Kamehameha—was not impressed. What did it matter that the horse could carry a person more quickly than the man could walk? Who would pay for all the food that the horse would have to be fed?

For a period of seven and a half years Cleveland wandered around the world, circling the globe twice. At the end of that time he parted from his friend Shaler and went home to Salem. He was then only thirty years old and had accumulated enough experiences to fill several lifetimes. He returned home with the sum of $70,000, a tidy fortune in his day.

But Cleveland's hope of retiring from the sea did not materialize. For many years afterward he crisscrossed the oceans of the world, as captain of trading ships, some profitable, some unprofitable.

Richard Cleveland died in 1860, eighty-seven years old. In his long lifetime he made several fortunes and lost them.

CHAPTER

"Adventurers" from Salem

SALEM SEA CAPTAINS filled the holds of their ships with pepper, coffee, and other exotic items to bring home, at the same time keeping a sharp lookout for anything that might tempt the Chinese. The United States was competing with the British, who could offer the Chinese opium, made from poppies growing in India, and strange soup ingredients, such as birds' nests and sharks' fins. As supplies of ginseng ran low, it became vital to the Americans to find something else that could be traded for teas, silks, and porcelains. The New Englanders came upon a prized soup-making ingredient—the *bêche-de-mer*, or sea slug, found on the coral reefs of the South Pacific.

Peirce-Nichols house, with a "captain's walk" on the roof, designed 1782 by Samuel McIntire for Salem shipping merchant

The slugs were also known as sea cucumbers, because of their shape. These little creatures, ranging in size from six to fifteen inches, were often gathered by the man-eating tribes of the South Sea islands. Dealing with these tribesmen added danger to the adventure and excitement of the Far Eastern trade.

But the perils of the China trade were more than balanced by the wealth it produced. In a few short years Salem was able to boast greater riches than nearby Boston. The Salem seaport became one of the busiest in the world, its wharves piled high with coffee and pepper, its waterfront crowded with sailors fresh from the East Indies.

As their wealth increased, the shipowners, merchants, and captains withdrew from Derby Street, which ran along the Salem waterfront. One of the best-known of America's house builders, Samuel McIntire, was called in to construct stately mansions on Chestnut and Essex streets. These houses had a railed walkway on the roof, where a shipowner would often stand, pointing his long telescope toward the sea, hoping to catch the first glimpse of a sail that could be bringing him either new fortune or ruin. The walkway came to be known as a "widow's walk," because of the women who went there to watch for their husbands, some of whom never returned.

During the day Salem shipmasters, strolling through the streets, might see another Far East trader walking toward the wharves, followed by a Chinese youth in bright silks. Or he might sit down to dinner in the local inn and be served by an East Indian wearing a colorful turban.

Salem's trade with the Orient, which included dealings not only with China but with all of the East Indies, suffered severely during the War of 1812, in which two-thirds of the port's fleet was destroyed. Salem's China traders abandoned the traffic, leaving only one of their number, Joseph Peabody, who continued sporadically until 1841.

But the magic of the Orient inspired the little New England seaport. Youngsters spent eager hours scanning the horizon for the first sight of a returning sail. When they saw one, they rushed into town to spread the news and claim a silver half-dollar from the excited owner. Some of the dollars found their way back to sea, reinvested in an "adventure" in Eastern seas.

CHAPTER *18*

Boston Makes Its Mark

SALEM'S SUCCESS DID not go unnoticed by shipowners and merchants in Boston, who were preparing to make their own bid for a share of the China and Far Eastern trade. Boston's earliest commercial dealings with the Orient were sponsored by Major Samuel Shaw, who had been involved with the pioneer voyage of the *Empress of China*. Shaw arranged with a group

Amaso Delano

of Boston merchants to back an ambitious venture. In 1789, in company with Captain Thomas Randall, he contracted for the largest commercial vessel built in America to that date, patterned after one of the big merchant ships of the British East India Company. The 800-ton vessel was appropriately named the *Massachusetts*.

Command of the ship was entrusted to Captain Job Prince. The crew consisted of four mates, a purser, a surgeon, a ship's carpenter, a gunner, four quartermasters, three midshipmen, a cooper, two cooks, a steward, and fifty able seamen. The second officer was Amaso Delano, who later became one of the famous captains in the China trade.

Even before the *Massachusetts* left Boston, she was beset by bad luck. A local fortune teller had predicted disaster for the vessel, and the crew that had been signed on promptly deserted. While the ship was still being built, two additional complements of men had to be recruited before the staff of officers and men was finally filled. The ship left Boston, headed for the Dutch East Indies port of Batavia. The course followed Shaw's previous voyages to China around the southern tip of Africa. But by the time the *Massachusetts* reached her destination, her hull, fashioned of unseasoned white oak, had rotted. In the hold a shipment of masts and spars had been stowed before the timber had been properly dried. The wood, covered with mud and ice, had decayed and fouled the air under the sealed hatches, spoiling several hundred barrels of beef.

The ship's misfortunes continued. In Batavia the partners, Shaw and Randall, were not permitted to engage in any commercial dealings because the Dutch had sealed the port. When they reached Canton, they found that prices for imported goods had dropped, leaving the New Englanders without enough money to repair the damage to the ship or to buy a suitable cargo for the return voyage. Their last recourse was to sell the ship. The officers and men scattered for home.

The failure of the venture of the *Massachusetts* made Boston's merchants cautious. They concluded that it would be better to risk less by using smaller ships with smaller cargo capacities, and they decided that they needed a trade item to substitute for lumber.

By the time ships from Boston became fully engaged in the China trade, more than a dozen American voyages to Canton from other ports had been completed.

Boston established its own place in the commerce with China. Its ships began traveling a different route to the Far East, rounding icy Cape Horn at the tip of South America rather than following in the wake of Salem and New York ships around Africa. Boston traders also decided to concentrate on a relatively new item for the market in China: the fur of the sea otter, which could be collected in great quantities on the Northwest Coast.

Sea-otter fur, thick, dark, and glossy, was highly esteemed in China, particularly by the senior officials of the Imperial Court, who wore it as coat linings or neckbands. A prime otter skin, perhaps four and a half feet long, was expensive, ranging as high in price as $70 a pelt.

For a long time the supply of the fur in China was limited, coming only from a few Russian traders operating in the Pacific Northwest. Even before the arrival of the Russians, the Indians of the Northwest had carried on an active trade with other native people, exchanging fish, candlefish oil, and shell for abalone from California, mountain-sheep horn, goat's wool, and furs from the interior, and copper from southern Alaska. Years of experience had taught the coastal people the intricacies of barter and exchange.

Trading for furs in the Pacific Northwest appealed to six Bostonians, who banded together to finance a venture in the China trade. Among them was Charles Bullfinch, the architect, who later became famous for

Fur-lined hood, fur coat and cap, worn by lady and attendant: hanging paper scroll by unknown Chinese artist, nineteenth century

The Columbia-Rediviva *and the sloop* Lady Washington: *illustration from journal of the voyage, by Robert Haswell*

designing the Boston State House and the first United States Capitol in Washington, D.C.

The Boston expedition consisted of two ships: the eleven-year-old *Columbia-Rediviva*, 212 tons, and the sloop *Lady Washington*, 90 tons, which was to serve as a tender, a ship small enough to get into coves and bays where larger vessels dared not venture. John Kendrick was named captain of the *Columbia*, as the ship was popularly known, and Robert Gray was given command of the *Lady Washington*. Both men had served on privateers during the American War for Independence. Both ships were heavily armed.

The Boston ships managed to sail together until they almost reached Cape Horn. In the south Atlantic Ocean they ran into heavy winds, towering seas, blinding snowstorms, and drifting icebergs, which forced the ships to part company. The two captains did not see each other again until they reached the fur-trading region near Vancouver, in what is now western Canada.

Almost a year had gone by since the ships had left Boston with cargoes of assorted trinkets: snuffboxes, rat traps, mouth organs, earrings, buttons, beads, and pocket mirrors, as well as iron tools. The Indians had learned to value iron, which they first discovered in the wreckage of ships washed up on their shores.

But by the time the Bostonians reached the Pacific Northwest, the fur-trading season was over. Months went by before the Indian hunters brought in new catches. In the meantime the captains and crews had to wait patiently, while their provisions dwindled.

Eventually a new season's supply of sea-otter fur became available, and trading between the Indians and the Bostonians picked up. An Indian trading session usually opened with festivities, perhaps a song, as the Indians paddled up to the ship. The leader or chief acted as spokesman for the entire group, who squatted silently before the furs which were displayed in their most favorable light. Often the choicest skins were hidden until a high enough price had been agreed upon. In later years a trade language developed called Chinook jargon, after one of the Indian groups of the Pacific Northwest. The trade talk consisted primarily of Chinook words, mixed with a few phrases in English and French.

By the time Captains Kendrick and Gray had traded the last of their iron tools and other items, the hold of the *Columbia* was full of sea-otter fur. In a switch of commands, Captain Gray took over on the bridge of the *Columbia* and set off westward across the Pacific for Canton. En route he put in at the Sandwich Islands—a welcome stopover, breaking the long sea voyage. There the ship could restock its stores with fresh meat, fowl, fruits, vegetables, and sugar, which varied the monotonous sea diet of dried beef.

The *Columbia* finally arrived at Macao, where a Chinese pilot was taken on. As with all other ships in the China trade, the *Columbia* proceeded up the Pearl River to the foreign ships' anchorage at Whampoa, where it was arranged to have the cargo of otter skins unloaded. The sale of the furs in Canton was brisk, and the *Columbia* assembled a cargo for home.

When she departed from Canton and set her course for Boston, she was sailing still westward, this time around the Cape of Good Hope. She became the first American vessel to navigate the globe completely.

An officer of the King of Hawaii: engraving by S. Leroy after Jacques E. V. Arago

Early on a sunny August afternoon in 1790, three years after she had set out, the *Columbia* was back in the inner harbor at Boston. The captain ordered the deck cannon fired in two thirteen-gun salutes, while the docks quickly filled with cheering onlookers. There was a special treat in store for the wide-eyed crowds— the sight of a native of the South Pacific, a prince of the Hawaiian Islands named Attoi, whom Captain Gray had brought back with him. The prince's shoulders were draped with a cape of yellow and scarlet feathers; a crested helmet on his head glittered in the sun.

The *Columbia*'s cargo proved to be less profitable in Boston than the ship's backers had hoped. The market was already glutted with Chinese goods brought back on the Salem ship *Astrea*, which had reached Massachusetts two months earlier.

Nevertheless, the Boston merchants did not let the *Columbia* linger in port. She was soon on the high seas again, headed for the Northwest Coast. On this second voyage Captain Gray, searching for sea-otter fur, came upon a great river, not marked on any of his charts, and he named it the Columbia River after his ship. In 1792 when Gray made his discovery, the Northwest Coast was not yet under the control of any of the European powers. The discovery of the Columbia River by Captain Gray became the basis on which the territory was claimed by the United States.

Besides the dangers of sailing in uncharted waters, American sea captains faced constant threats of attack from the Indians. They could never be certain about what the reaction would be to an offer to trade, so the overseas visitors came ready to pit gunpowder and firearms against primitive stone spears, wooden clubs, and bows and arrows. Often a trading ship would find herself surrounded by Indians in large war canoes, some of which were larger than the sailing craft. The coastal people, crowding around the trading ship in dugout canoes, usually outnumbered the foreign crew, so boardings nets were thrown over the ship's side to allow only a few Indians on board at one time. Meanwhile men

Kwakiutl Indians in ceremonial dress: photograph by Edward S. Curtis, 1914

armed with muskets and blunderbusses were stationed in the crosstrees to guard the ship if the Indians proved to be unfriendly.

Each ship had swivel guns on her bulwarks, as well as cannon, usually loaded and ready to be fired. Along the quarterdecks were loopholes for musket fire.

Nevertheless, every encounter was filled with peril for the overseas traders. Escape from attack could be made only under sail, and there was always danger of a calm—with no wind to blow the ship to safety. There was also the possibility of a submerged reef or unseen rock, on which a vessel might become helplessly immobilized in the face of an assault.

Gray had brought with him for his second visit to the Northwest Coast a varied assortment of articles that proved attractive to the Indians, particularly sheets of copper which they highly valued. Gray also carried pieces of blue, red, and green blanket material, called duffils, as well as bright red cloth. He brought 4261 chisels, each weighing a quarter of a pound, 150 pairs of shoes, worth 75 cents apiece, blue woolen trousers,

The Columbia *being attacked by Northwest Coast Indians: illustration from journal of the voyage, by George Davidson*

worth 92 cents each, pea jackets, greatcoats, watch coats, and fearnoughts,—a stout cloth worn as an outer garment at sea. Also in the cargo were quantities of buttons, 14,000 iron nails, and 100 old muskets and blunderbusses. In addition, the ship carried hogsheads of rum, which was used in trading with the Indians.

Gray's judgment on his second voyage proved more profitable than on his first. After three years at sea he brought his ship home to Boston with a cargo from China that produced a profit of $90,000.

CHAPTER *19*

Boston's Captains and Merchants

THE SUCCESSFUL VOYAGES of the *Columbia* inspired other Bostonians. Two of them, Captain James

Chinese coin headdress worn by Indian girl: photograph by Edward S. Curtis, 1910

Magee and his young brother-in-law, Thomas Handasyd Perkins, had already been to Canton on the *Astrea*, out of Salem. Magee and Perkins purchased a 70-ton brigantine, the *Hope*, and hired as captain Joseph Ingraham, one of the mates from the *Columbia*. Ingraham took aboard a supply of bright cloth, which he planned to trade for sea-otter fur. His route was around Cape Horn, following the path of the *Columbia*. Unfortunately, when he reached the Northwest Coast, he found the Indians reluctant to deal with him. They did not seem to want any more cloth from New England. Captain Ingraham solved his problem by having bright brass buttons sewn onto the cloth, which was immediately accepted by the Indians. Ingraham made collars of iron nails, which also appealed to the Northwest Coast people. Each collar was traded for three otter skins.

After filling his brigantine with furs, Ingraham sailed for China. When he reached Canton, he found to his dismay that the trading price for each skin was lower

Trade buttons outline the body and features of a seated bear: blanket made by Tsimshian Indians of Northwest Coast

than he had expected. Nevertheless, he managed to dispose of his cargo at a profit. He invested the proceeds in a full cargo of Chinese goods, mostly tea, which he sent back to Boston in a homebound vessel. Ingraham sailed back to the Northwest Coast to continue dealing with the Indians. But there he found that other captains had copied his idea of trading iron collars for furs. More collars were available than the Indians could use.

———————— ◆ ————————

Some of Boston's leading figures in the China trade went to sea as youngsters, becoming captains while they were still in their teens. Some won additional attention by publishing accounts of their travels and exploits.

John Boit, Jr., was still a youth when he sailed as a captain's mate on the *Columbia* on its voyage around the world. He wrote a narrative of his adventures, which he also illustrated. Boit was one of the first Americans to describe Hawaii and its people.

While still in his teens, Boit was named the master of a 60-foot sloop, the *Union*, 89 tons, in which he set out from Newport, Rhode Island, for his second journey to the Far East. He had a cargo of copper, iron, and cloth to trade for furs on the Northwest Coast. After dealing with the Indians for several months, he sailed for Canton by way of Hawaii. From China the young captain continued westward, bringing the *Union* home around the globe. His was the first sloop to circumnavigate the earth.

William Sturgis, another Boston lad, was a sea captain when he was only nineteen. He had gone to sea for the first time when he was fourteen. At twenty-eight, he founded the firm Bryant and Sturgis, which became one of Boston's most active traders with China.

Young Sturgis had exciting experiences with pirates in Oriental seas. One encounter took place practically inside the harbor at Macao, as he was bringing in his ship *Atahualpa*, named after the Inca leader of Peru. Sturgis's ship with a full cargo, plus $300,000 in silver, had just come through some of the worst pirate-infested seas in the world. The youthful captain was heaving a sigh of

The sloop Union *returning to Boston: illustration from journal of the voyage by Captain John Boit, Jr.*

relief as he reached Lark's Bay at the mouth of the Pearl River. Now he was within the protection of the Portuguese forts at Macao. Confidently he sent his mate, Daniel C. Bacon, to arrange for a Chinese pilot to guide him up the river.

As he waited for the mate to come back with the pilot, Sturgis spied a fleet of Chinese pirate junks bearing down on him. Some of the pirate ships were twice the size of the Boston vessel, which lay in the water practically becalmed. Sturgis had several cannon aboard, despite orders from the shipowners that he carry no heavy armament. The guns were made ready and a warning shot fired in the hope that the attackers would be frightened away. But they pressed on relentlessly toward the drifting ship. Sturgis threatened to blow up his ship and the pirates as well if they dared to board his vessel, but they kept coming, intent on overwhelming the Americans. While the Bostonians were fighting off the pirates, a light wind came up and the ship began to move very slowly. The struggle raged on as both the ship and the

attackers drifted toward Macao. When they were within range of the Portuguese forts, the harbor cannon opened fire and demolished the pirate fleet. The event was witnessed by thousands lined up along the shore.

A report of Sturgis's narrow escape came to the attention of the ship's owners, one of whom, Theodore Lyman, commented: "Hadn't we ordered you not to carry cannon!" The story is told that Lyman, as a lesson in obedience, ordered freight charges levied against the captain for carrying the cannon.

As dozens of ships, mostly from Boston, appeared in the Pacific Northwest, the supply of sea-otter fur began to diminish. Between 1795 and 1804 a total of sixty-eight ships were engaged in collecting cargoes of sea-otter pelts. In the year 1800 alone sixteen vessels competed with one another for the dwindling supply. The sharp rivalry among the traders led to bitter dealings with the Indians and to the near extinction of the fur-bearing animals.

A new source of sea-otter fur was needed to supple-ment the decreasing cargoes from the Northwest Coast, and Boston ships began exploring the inlets and bays of the California shore. The first American vessel to establish contact between the eastern United States and the territory of California was the Boston ship, appropriately named the *Otter*, captained by Ebenezer Dorr.

For a few years cargoes of sea-otter fur could be taken on in California for sale in Canton. But soon the supply of fur in California also diminished, to be replaced by other trade articles. Cargoes of animal hides and tallow were loaded on board in Monterey, Santa Barbara, and San Diego, and exchanged in Canton for tea, silk, porcelain, lacquered writing desks, and other Chinese commodities. China traders from Boston developed commercial links with California, which helped lead to its admission to the United States in 1850 as the thirty-first state.

For several decades during the first half of the nineteenth century, the leading Bostonian in Canton was John Perkins Cushing, nephew of Thomas Handasyd

A pirate ship at Canton

Home of Captain Robert Bennett Forbes, built in 1833, now the Museum of the American China Trade, Milton, Massachusetts

Perkins and James Perkins. Cushing, who had been sent to China at the age of sixteen, was just beginning to learn the rudiments of trading with the hong merchants when his superior suddenly died. Young Cushing found himself in charge of his uncles' sizable operations. Back in Boston one of the elder Perkinses was preparing to set sail for Canton to take charge of the situation, when it became apparent that the nephew had the business fairly well in hand. Cushing represented the Perkins Company in China for twenty years. During that time he won good friends among the Cantonese, many of whom called him Ku-shing. When he returned to Boston, Cushing tried to re-create the life he had known in the Far East. His garden was enclosed by a porcelain wall. Inside, peacocks and mandarin ducks strutted near a pond filled with lotus flowers.

Many relatives of Thomas Handasyd Perkins profited from the China trade. Three brothers, Thomas Tunno Forbes, Robert Bennett Forbes, and John Murray Forbes, were Perkins' nephews. The Forbes brothers were active in Russell and Company, which succeeded their uncle's firm in 1838. Thomas Tunno was killed in China. His two younger brothers continued in the trade and used their profits to finance railroad construction and shipbuilding in the United States.

Another important Boston firm was operated by James and Thomas Lamb. One of their ships, the *Hazard*, is said to have gathered the largest collection of furs ever taken to China from the Northwest Coast.

Many of Boston's leading China traders began their careers as sea captains. Augustine Heard's life was peppered with narrow escapes from shipwreck and from attacks by pirates. Heard was a crusty ship's captain who became a hardheaded merchant. After helping to make Russell and Company the largest American firm in China, Heard became dissatisfied with the company and left to form his own organization, which soon was almost as large and as important as the one he had left.

Other Bostonians whose wealth was founded on commerce with China included the Cabots, the Appletons,

Boston harbor from Constitution Wharf: painting by Robert Salmon, about 1842

the Sampsons, and the Tappans. One trader was named Supply Clap Thwing.

For a while, during the early years of the nineteenth century, Boston maintained a position of leadership in the American–China trade, rivaling both Philadelphia and New York. When Salem's share of the commerce with Canton declined, Boston's merchants continued their activities. After 1815, even as New York developed into the major receiving port in the United States for all goods from China, Boston sometimes sent more ships to Canton than any of its competitors. But many Boston ships, before returning to their home port, sailed past Sandy Hook and unloaded their cargoes on New York wharves.

Trading with China and other Far Eastern ports resulted in some unusual examples of Yankee ingenuity. A young Bostonian, Frederic Tudor, at work as a shipping clerk in the sweltering heat of the West Indies, kept thinking of cold crisp New England winters and the thick ice covering the ponds near his home. "How cooling an iced drink would be in the heat of a tropical port!" Tudor thought.

Tudor returned to Boston with his idea, only to find himself greeted with loud guffaws of laughter. Sell ice? Who would buy it? No one ever had! However, young Tudor was not one to abandon a good idea so easily. He experimented with ways to insulate the ice so that it could be shipped over long distances, even into the heat of the tropics. He finally hit upon sawdust as the ideal insulating material to keep the ice from melting in transit. He worked over designs for special ships, some with double hulls that could provide insulation for a cargo of ice.

Then Tudor bought the rights to cut the ice on dozens of ponds and lakes near Boston. He put up buildings in various places in the tropics, in which to store the ice. Since ice was unknown in the warm climates, Tudor had first to demonstrate how refrigerated foods were kept from spoiling and how cooled drinks could be especially refreshing. Once a demand for ice had been created, he shipped thousands of tons of it to the West Indies, San Francisco, Persia, and even to India.

"Does the strange stuff [ice] grow on trees or shrubs?" was a question asked of Tudor in India.

By the middle of the nineteenth century he was shipping 150,000 tons of ice a year to various parts of the world.

CHAPTER 20

Sailing Ships and Cotton Mills

"If I should never Venter [venture] nothing, I should Never have nothing." These words, spoken in 1736 by Captain Obadiah Brown of Providence, Rhode Island, expressed an underlying force behind the development of the China trade. Brown, a shipmaster in Colonial times, was the father of a family of four brothers, who played a prominent role in America's commerce with China.

The Browns differed from most other New England China traders in their preference for large ships, with great cargo-carrying capacities. Providence's waterfront was developed to handle the large vessels. Canals were dug, wharves built, and shipyards erected in what came to be known as India Point.

The port of Providence had not always been Rhode Island's main outlet to the sea. In Colonial times the most important shipping center had been Newport. But the occupation of Newport by the British during all the years of the Revolutionary War had driven away American shipping interests, and they never went back.

In 1787, three years after the *Empress of China* opened the China trade for America, John Brown of Providence launched his first ship destined for trading in the Pacific

Ocean. The ship, a 1000-ton vessel, was named the *General Washington*. President George Washington himself was present at the launching.

With Captain Jonathan Donnison in command, the *General Washington* cleared for the Far East, carrying a mixed cargo of ginseng, cannon shot, bar iron, iron anchors, tar, and a variety of alcoholic beverages. Ten months later the ship was in China, after putting in along the way at the Madeira Islands, St. Helena, Ascension, St. Eustatius, and India. The ship's voyage totaled 32,000 miles and ended back in Rhode Island in July 1789 with a cargo of tea, silk, chinaware, cotton goods, lacquerware, flannel cloth, and gloves.

Two years later, in 1791, Brown launched another large ship, which he named the *President Washington*. A contemporary report of the launching described how the ship "moved majestically from the Slips amidst the Plaudits of an immense Concourse of Spectators, among whom was a brilliant assemblage of the fair Daughters of America."

Naming two ships in honor of the first President of the United States was not enough for John Brown. He expressed his admiration with still a third vessel, which he called simply *George Washington*.

Another thriving Providence firm was originally founded by Nicholas Brown, Jr., and George Benson. Later it added the third name of Ives to its title, when Brown's daughter, Hope, set her heart on young Thomas Poynton Ives of Beverly, Massachusetts. Hope's father did not want her to marry the young man; he objected to the fact that Ives came from a family with little means. He would, he said, have preferred his daughter to marry a gentleman.

"Father, what makes a gentleman?" asked Hope.

"Money and manners!" was her father's reply.

"Well, Father, you have the money and Tom has the manners," said Hope. The elder Brown had just enough manners to withdraw his objections.

Brown, Benson, and Ives commissioned a new ship for the China trade, named *John Jay*, which sailed from

Providence on December 28, 1794, loaded with pig iron, bar iron, rum, gin, port wine, candy, tobacco, and other articles. The cargo was valued at $34,550. A little more than a year later, on January 16, 1796, the ship left Canton and headed back to Providence with a cargo worth a quarter of a million dollars. In 1806 the *John Jay* ran aground in a snowstorm and was lost with a valuable cargo.

Another of the firm's ships, the *Eliza*, was wrecked off the Fiji Islands in 1808. The captain, Charles Savage, rather than return to Rhode Island, chose to join one of the native tribes, the Bau. Eventually he became a leader of these South Sea island people.

As more and more ships competed in the China trade, speed became increasingly important for success. The first shipments to reach the market usually commanded the highest prices. In 1798 the firm, now called Brown and Ives, commissioned a ship, named for the wives of the two owners, the *Ann and Hope*, which became one of the speediest vessels in the service. On her maiden voyage she reached Canton from Providence in five months and one day, then covered the homeward distance in 126 days—just over four months. The *Ann and Hope* sailed back and forth between Providence and Canton many times. On one trip her supercargo was Samuel Snow, who remained in Canton to become the second American consul in the Chinese port, following Samuel Shaw.

Another American consul in Canton (1802–1811) was Edward Carrington, who took over the China trade in Providence after 1815. Carrington's shipping firm in Rhode Island had a fleet of twenty-six vessels, trading in all parts of the globe. Carrington built a mansion that is still standing in Providence. Along its roof is a railed walkway, which afforded him a sweeping view of the harbor and his incoming ships.

For the next few decades numerous vessels set sail from

The ship George Washington, *built in 1793: painting by* *Thomas Chambers, mid-nineteenth century*

Providence, bound for China. In a single year, 1819, five ships came back from Canton to the Rhode Island port. But the China trade from Providence was soon in a decline. Each year fewer and fewer ships were engaged in the commerce, and for several seasons not one ship plied the seas between Rhode Island and the foreign anchorage at Whampoa in the Pearl River.

Some of the Brown family profits from the China trade were invested in manufacturing in New England. Moses Brown became interested in a cotton mill in Pawtucket, Rhode Island, the first successful cotton manufacturing plant in the United States. In a few years the Pawtucket factory was turning out inexpensive cotton cloth, driving out of the American market the handmade nankeens that had been imported from China.

Other cotton mills and textile plants were founded in New England with money made from the import of tea. Machine-made cotton textiles poured out of these factories in an increasing flood, some of it even going as an export to China.

CHAPTER *21*

Sails, Seals, and Sandalwood

THE SEARCH FOR goods that could be exchanged in the market at Canton took American sailors literally to the ends of the earth, even to the inhospitable islands of the South Seas, where the fur seal abounded.

Seal fur was highly prized at Canton, where the pelts were first introduced almost as an afterthought. A Nantucket ship, the *States*, had come to New York from the Falkland Islands with 13,000 sealskins. But no one in New York knew just what to do with them. The price offered was only fifty cents a skin. In the hope that the furs might fetch a better price in China, the entire shipload was sent off. The furs were taken to Canton on the brig *Eleanora*, under Captain Simon Metcalf. At Canton the price was multiplied ten times, skyrocketing to five dollars per skin. Here indeed was new treasure!

Almost immediately a race got under way to find the barren outposts used by the southern fur seals as breeding grounds. Every year the seals returned to the lonely rocks where they had always been safe from predators. Some of these islands were isolated outcroppings in the South Atlantic, including the Falkland Islands, Patagonia, Tierra del Fuego, and snow-covered South Georgia Island. Others were in the Pacific, thousands of miles away. One of the most important in the Pacific area was off the western coast of South America, an island of the Juan Fernandez group, called Más Afuera—meaning in Portuguese "more to sea." In the southern reaches of the Indian Ocean were Crozet Islands, Prince Edward Island, Kerguelen, McDonald, and Heard Islands.

The seal was an offshoot of the bear family and had once been a land animal before becoming adapted to life in the sea. Two species of seal were to be found on the southern islands: the fur seal and the hair seal. The hair seal was larger than the fur seal. Its pelt had no value in Canton, although there was a market for it in America and Europe. The fur seal has a soft, shiny undercoat. It was used as a lining for winter coats by the lower ranks of Chinese nobility and the lesser grades of government officials.

A male fur seal measured from three to six feet in length. His coat was normally a dark brown fur. A female was usually half the size, with a dark silver-gray coat. When the female reached the breeding ground, she was swept up into a harem that might include a dozen others, presided over by a fierce, ever-watchful male. Soon the pups, carried by their mothers since the previous season, were born, each weighing about six pounds, each a bundle of black fur.

At first the seal hunters were able to fill the holds of their ships in only a few months, sometimes from the breeding grounds on a single island. Later, as more hunters pursued the dwindling herds, a sealing gang would have to spend two or even three lonely years in order to collect enough skins to fill a ship.

A sealing crew in the Falkland Islands

A seal-hunting gang ranged in size from twenty to thirty men. Some of the crewmen were inexperienced youngsters from farms near the American seaports where the ships originated. Many sealing crews also included British convicts, who had been sent to penal colonies in Australia and had either served out their sentences or escaped.

To hunt the seals the crew came ashore on the island and formed a line between the seals and the escape route to the sea. The men, armed with clubs, advanced slowly and struck the seals, stunning them with a blow. After the seals were killed with a knife, the fur was removed. The pelts were cleaned and washed in preparation for stretching and drying.

Sealers made use of the fur to provide themselves with warm clothing, mocassins, blankets, door curtains, and roof coverings. The flesh of the seal served as food. One man, named Daniel Foss, was shipwrecked on a desolate seal island a half mile long. For five years he survived on a diet of seal meat, the only food available. Another story of survival on an island in the South Pacific concerns Captain Charles Barnard of Hudson, New York. Captain Barnard, commanding the brig *Nanina*, 132 tons, came upon a group of Englishmen who had been stranded when their crew mutinied. Captain Barnard went off to gather some food for the castaways and returned to find that the British had sailed off in his ship. Barnard and his men survived for years on a diet of seal meat.

The key roles in developing the trade in sealskins were played by Connecticut captains. The very first direct voyage to the sealing grounds was undertaken in 1790 by Captain Daniel Greene of New Haven, who led an expedition of two ships, the *Nancy* and the *Polly*. That same year a ship from Philadelphia, the *Industry*, collected a cargo of 5600 sealskins.

Six years later, in 1796, Captain Greene set sail from his Connecticut port in command of the *Neptune*, 350 tons, with a crew of forty-five men. At the Falkland Islands he had his ship's carpenter build a small open boat, a 30-ton shallop, which was left behind with the sealing gang, while the mother ship sailed on for other ports. The shallop was used to get into the narrow coves and inlets along the rocky coast, to put the men ashore where they could climb up the steep slopes. By the time Captain Green came back with the *Neptune*, the crewmen had collected 30,000 pelts.

Greene filled the hold of the *Neptune* with the furs and headed for China around Cape Horn. The voyage took place in bitter winter weather, with the ship's decks piled high with snow, its rigging caked with ice. There was a ready market for the sealskins at Canton.

For the return voyage of the *Neptune* a cargo was assembled consisting of 1200 chests of tea, among them America's favorite types: Bohea, Hyson, Hyson Skin, and Souchong. On the homeward trip the ship circled the globe, sailing around the Cape of Good Hope. On July 11, 1799, Captain Greene dropped anchor in the harbor at New Haven, Connecticut. The *Neptune* and its crew had been away for almost three years.

The Fannings of Stonington, Connecticut, were probably the most active family in the sealing trade. There were eight Fanning boys, all of whom went to sea in search of new breeding grounds of the fur seal. When one of the Fannings found an isolated spot in the South Seas that the seals favored, he would leave a note for one of his brothers in a private hiding place to inform him of the new rookery.

Captain Edmund Fanning led about seventy voyages to the South Seas and to China. Most of them were backed by merchants in New York. During one voyage on the *Betsy*, en route to Canton with a cargo of sealskins, he was attacked off the island of Sumatra by a fleet of twenty-nine seagoing craft. The boats, called *proas*, were manned by Malays. Despite her small size the 93-ton *Betsy* carried a crew of thirty men and was rigged to look like a man-of-war. Guns were painted on her sides to give the vessel a formidable appearance, but the pirates were not fooled. They pressed the attack against

The Betsy: *lithograph, 1833*

the sluggish vessel, overloaded with sealskins. There were ten real cannon on board, which were loaded with round shot and bags of musket balls. When the Malay pirates swept within musket-shot of the Connecticut ship, the cannon roared, driving off the marauders with two murderous broadsides.

At the height of his activities as a sealer, Captain Fanning had a fleet of twelve small ships, which together totaled only 850 tons. The crews required to man the entire fleet consisted of only 202 officers and men.

The Connecticut captains sailed into unknown waters in the southern seas and put in at islands that did not appear on any maps. Captain Edmund Fanning was almost shipwrecked on a small island in the Pacific, now known as Fanning Island. He also discovered nearby the islands of Washington and Palmyra, two thousand miles south of Hawaii.

Another Stonington captain, Benjamin Morrell, was aboard the schooner *Antarctica* in 1829 when he came upon an unknown group of islands, which he named

Bergh's Group. Morrell had given up searching for seal rookeries and had turned to trading in sandalwood and sea slugs when he made his discoveries of new South Sea islands. He was one of the first to popularize the romance of the South Pacific, in spite of the fact that his dealings with the islanders involved cruelty and treachery.

About 1844 Captain Morrell was in command of a new ship, the *Margaret Oakley*, out of New York, to Canton. But on his way back to New York the ship disappeared, without a trace. For many years legends floated about the South Seas concerning Captain Morrell and a colony he was supposed to have founded. In reality, his ship had been wrecked off the coast of Madagascar and the captain had turned back to the South Seas as a passenger on another ship. Somewhere along the way he died or was lost, for he was never heard of again.

Seal-hunting expeditions from America scoured the southern seas, searching for the animals on every island. The ships sailed into the frigid Antarctic regions, as well as the tropical Galápagos, which lie along the equator off the western coast of South America. However, the seals in the South Seas could not breed fast enough to outlive the annual slaughter. Within a few years the islands were depleted. But Captain Fanning never really gave up. At the age of seventy-one he was still actively trying to persuade the Federal government to sponsor new expeditions to discover untouched seal islands in the Antarctic.

◆ ◆ ◆

Nathaniel Palmer was probably the most famous of the Stonington captains to sail out of New York. He had all the basic instincts of a sailor; he could feel his way through darkness and fog. Palmer was only fourteen years old when he first went to sea. He was a member of the crew of an American ship that slipped in and out of harbors blockaded by the British in the War of 1812.

When he was eighteen years old, Palmer signed on as the second mate of the *Hersilia* for a voyage to the seal islands of the South Atlantic. Antarctic waters were dangerous for sailing ships. Uncharted reefs just below the ocean surface could rip out a ship's bottom. Huge icebergs were a constant peril. The winds howled, churning the seas into mountains of water. Ships' rigging stiffened with coatings of ice. Near the southern end of the globe, the magnetic pole, unknown to the early navigators, caused compass needles to spin wildly, making it difficult to determine direction. Much of the time dense fog shrouded the ships, the sea, and the sky, rendering navigating instruments useless. Palmer's instincts for navigating blindly at sea proved exceedingly useful.

By the time he was twenty-one, Palmer was a captain, in command of a little sloop, the *Hero*, designed to scout for new seal islands. His two mates were also twenty-one, and one of his crewmen was a lad of sixteen. The oldest seaman aboard was thirty-one, Peter Harvey, a black American.

Untouched breeding grounds had to be found as hunters were overrunning the known islands. The first sealing ship to reach the South Shetlands had been able to collect 9000 skins on the island. A year later thirty ships had converged on the same spot. Palmer was sent off in the *Hero* to find new breeding sites.

As he sailed farther into the ice-studded sea, he encountered great banks of fog rolling in from the horizon. One morning, with the sky still overcast, albatross and Mother Carey's chickens suddenly appeared overhead. Gulls came screaming in over his masts. Land had to be close at hand.

Through an opening in the mist a high wall of black rock came into view. Ice-capped, the rock wall encircled a bay, in which the ocean steamed and bubbled. Palmer had come upon the crater of a partly submerged volcano, still active. The volcano's underground fires kept the water hot in spite of the icebergs that tumbled down from the edges of the glacier along the overhanging rim of rock. Palmer and his crew enjoyed a warm bath.

Two days later, in November 1820, the young captain reached an island on which a high peak rose. Palmer climbed to the top and saw in the distance for the first time the snow-clad mountains of Antarctica. The continent he was looking at was not marked on any of the navigation charts then known. For a long time the continent was called Palmer's Land. One of Antarctica's landmarks is still known as Palmer's Peninsula.

In later years Nathaniel Palmer became one of the most popular captains of the American clipper ships, which he helped design. One clipper ship was named the *N.B. Palmer* in his honor.

———◆———

The more the seal hunters roamed the southern seas, the more breeding grounds they came upon and depleted. Traders soon had to find another item with which to continue their commerce with China.

Simon Metcalf, captain of the brig *Eleanora*, found sandalwood growing in Hawaii and carried a shipment to Canton. Sandalwood is a fragrant tree that grows high in the hills above the barrier reefs around some of the islands of the South Seas. The sandalwood tree contains an inner core that is aromatic and has no grain, which makes it ideal for carving. Because the odor repels insects, the wood is widely used for chests and cabinets. The dust of the wood was compressed into wands or tapers, called joss sticks, which were burned in Chinese ceremonials, emitting a pungent odor.

In 1804 sandalwood was discovered in the Fiji Islands. A year later a sealing captain, Peter Chase, brought the first load to China on board his ship, the *Criterion*, out of Nantucket. The cargo of sandalwood, for which Captain Chase had exchanged trinkets worth $1500, brought a shipload of silk and tea valued at $80,000.

Almost immediately ships from New York, Boston, and Salem headed for Vanua Levu on the Fiji Islands where the sandalwood grew. The sandalwood route was generally by way of Australia, where the ships put in to sell rum, gin, brandy, and wine. The Fiji Islanders themselves valued most highly whales' teeth, which were believed to possess magical powers. Old, darkened whales' teeth, which averaged about a pound in weight, were especially prized as neck ornaments, brides' dowries, or sacred offerings to the gods. Less desirable, but still accepted, in trade for sandalwood, were metal knife blades, glass bottles, mirrors, beads, buttons, needles, nails, and colored cotton cloth.

The supply of sandalwood in Hawaii was controlled by the king, Kamehameha I. In 1811 he agreed to grant the sole right to all the sandalwood on his islands to three ships' captains, Jonathan Winship and his brother, Nathan, and William Davis, all originally from Boston. The Americans transferred their three ships, the *O'Cain*, the *Albatross*, and the *Isabella*, to Hawaii, where they became known as the "Lords of the Pacific."

The trade in sandalwood in the Fiji Islands continued for just seven years. The trees grew only on the islands of Vanua Levu and were claimed as the sole property of the local chief. But the leaders of the other people on the islands in the Fiji group could not contain their jealousy of the wealth pouring in and decided to demand a share. The deadly rivalries of the native chieftains added to the perils of the sandalwood trade.

In 1807 and again in 1808 Edmund Fanning sent ships

to Fiji. Captain Reuben Brumley commanded both voyages. One of the last American ships to take on sandalwood for China was the *Hunter*, which originated in Boston. About $800 worth of trinkets were exchanged for sandalwood, which sold for $80,000 in Canton.

In a few years practically all the sandalwood trees on the South Sea islands were cut down. Then the War of 1812 between England and the United States, which drove American ships from the Pacific Ocean, finally put an end to America's stake in the sandalwood trade.

CHAPTER *22*

The Baltimore Clippers

THE CHESAPEAKE BAY port of Baltimore was opened to the China trade on August 12, 1785, when Captain John O'Donnell sailed into port on the *Pallas*, direct from Canton. The *Pallas*, which had been chartered by Thomas Randall, assistant supercargo of the *Empress of China*, brought in a full cargo of tea, as well as assorted porcelain.

While arrangements were being made to dispose of the Chinese merchandise, Captain O'Donnell and his crew went ashore to look over the city. The seamen were, for the most part, Chinese, Malay, Japanese, and Moors, and they appeared on the streets wearing native costumes. Their appearance proved a sensation.

A few days after the arrival of the *Pallas*, word reached Baltimore from George Washington that "if great bargains are to be had," he would like to obtain some sets of the finest chinaware, as well as some bowls, basins, jugs, and mugs. There is no record that his requests were filled.

Captain O'Donnell decided to establish his home port in Baltimore and soon became an American citizen. He married a young Baltimore woman and bought a handsome estate, which he named "Canton."

View of Baltimore from Federal Hill: lithograph by Fitz Hugh Lane

In 1786 another O'Donnell vessel, the *Chesapeake*, became one of the first American ships to begin trading with India. Just three years later, however, the *Chesapeake* returned from Canton, ending the last voyage of an O'Donnell ship in the China trade.

Shipbuilders along the banks of Chesapeake Bay soon realized the value of speed in getting overseas goods back to the home market. In Baltimore shipyards a small, fast-sailing ship was developed which set many records for swift passage to the Far East and return. The vessels became known as Baltimore clippers. Although the Baltimore clippers were speedy ships, they did not have sufficiently large cargo capacity to make their service a profitable undertaking.

In 1832 a ship of the new design, the *Ann McKim*, was launched in a Baltimore shipyard. Her lines were long; her masts leaned jauntily. The ship's hull gleamed with a sheath of copper; her decks glistened with brasswork and polished mahogany trim. Overhead the ship carried great expanses of billowing sails.

CHAPTER 23

Philadelphia Sends Its Ships

FIFTY MILES INLAND from the Atlantic Ocean, along the banks of the Delaware River, stands the city of Philadelphia, the busiest port in America during the first years of the Republic.

Philadelphia is located in the heart of rich farmland, which quickly attracted settlers to Pennsylvania. William Penn's colony included Quaker farmers, who made the soil yield bountiful crops. Non-Quakers also were among the grain farmers, and soon they, too, were reaping overflowing harvests. There was enough grain to fill all local needs, as well as to provide a surplus for shipment back to London, often in vessels that belonged to the farmers.

The port of Philadelphia: engraving, 1778

Among these first farming and trading families, some of whose members were Quakers, were the Walns, the Latimers, and the Donaldsons. Before long Quakers on both sides of the Atlantic Ocean became associated with one another, establishing a transatlantic pattern in which trade flourished. With little delay Philadelphia merchants became familiar with the mechanics of international trade. There was also a group of Jewish families in Philadelphia who had ties in various countries of Europe and who were able to open up additional trading avenues. These families, named Graetz, Marx, and Levy, were well-known in the Philadelphia community.

But as the trade from Philadelphia grew in volume, mercantile houses for shipping grain sprang up. The new group of merchants included Robert Morris, Thomas Willing, and Stephen Girard.

Robert Morris had already sponsored the *Empress of China*, which had made the first American voyage to Canton. He also had helped launch Philadelphia's pioneering journey to the Far East with a ship appropriately

named the *Canton*. In addition, he was involved with the *Asia*, 292 tons, the first ship in the China trade to be built in a Philadelphia yard. Morris, together with seventeen partners, backed her maiden voyage.

Inspired by Morris, Philadelphia merchants forged ahead in the trade with China, exporting and importing more goods than traders in any other Atlantic port. In 1809 thirteen ships from the Delaware River arrived in Canton. Before the War of 1812 Philadelphia merchants accounted for fully one-third of all trading activity between America and China.

One of Philadelphia's leading merchants, Stephen Girard, set up his warehouses and business headquarters on what came to be known as India Wharf. From there his ships set off on journeys that lasted for many months. Their long, meandering voyages might include a stop at a port along the south Atlantic coast for cotton or rice to be carried across the Atlantic to Europe and sold for silver dollars; then on to the Pacific to Canton for tea and silk, or to the Dutch or French islands for spices or

Delaware River front, Philadelphia: watercolor by Thomas Birch

Stephen Girard on the Philadelphia waterfront: painting by Frederick James (1885)

sugar, which would be brought back to Europe to be sold for more silver dollars. The ships finally returned to Philadelphia with the money, which went into Girard's bank—the first private banking organization in the country.

Girard admired the new scientific spirit of his day and especially the works of the French writers. In 1795 he ordered four ships built, which he named the *Voltaire*, the *Rousseau*, the *Montesquieu*, and the *Helvetius*. But for all his wealth Girard seemed lonely, with a wife who was hospitalized for twenty-five years, and no children. On his death in 1831 he left much of his fortune for the beautification of Philadelphia and for a college for orphans, which is still in operation.

With Girard gone from the scene, Philadelphia slipped behind New York in the number of ships heading out each year for Canton.

Profits from the China trade were sometimes invested in enterprises related to the commerce itself, such as shipbuilding. Other businesses had no direct connection, the

The Montesquieu, *owned by Stephen Girard: oil painting*

returns going to finance textile mills, build railroads, develop coal fields, or speculate in land.

The nearby city of Wilmington, Delaware, shared some of the benefits of Philadelphia's commerce with China. John Richardson Latimer started in the China trade as a young man on the Philadelphia ship, the *Benjamin Rush*. After years in Canton he returned to a great house in Wilmington, which he filled with Chinese furnishings and decorations.

Philadelphia exported large quantities of grain to Europe. In order to keep this commerce going without interruption, Philadelphia merchants needed an item that could be sold in China and yet would not interfere with the traffic to Europe. Ginseng, sea-otter fur, sealskins, sandalwood, exotic soup ingredients, and the other usual items did not fit conveniently into Philadelphia's pattern. An appropriate item soon became apparent—the extract of the poppy, which the British grew in India. Derived from the poppy were opium, heroin, and laudanum, all of which were widely used as medicines and painkillers.

The British permitted Americans to carry some of the drug home, but they forbade any of it to be transported to China.

In the late 1790s new fields of poppies were found in the vicinity of Smyrna, Turkey. Here was a source of opium outside the control of the British, and Americans were quick to exploit it. In 1804 the brig *Pennsylvania*, out of Philadelphia, touched at Smyrna and took on fifty chests of opium. The supercargoes on the brig were Benjamin Chew Wilcocks and his younger brother, James. The *Pennsylvania* did not carry her cargo of opium all the way to China but unloaded it at Batavia. The first American ship actually to bring opium to Canton was the Baltimore brig *Entan*, which arrived in 1806 with forty-six chests and fifty-three boxes of the drug. In July of the same year James Wilcocks arrived in Canton aboard the *Sylph*, which was carrying thirty-three cases of opium on board.

Opium met all of the criteria required by the merchants of Philadelphia for trading with China without interfering with their existing commercial operations with Europe. The drug was in constant demand by the Chinese. It was not very bulky, and required only limited shipping space in a vessel's hold. Use of the drug inside China seemed to be increasing, and the price was high and could be expected to remain high.

There was one difficulty. It was illegal to import opium into China.

CHAPTER 24

Illegal Opium

Opium was used in China originally as a drug to reduce pain, ease tensions, and induce sleep. Smoking opium for pleasure did not become a common addiction until the seventeenth and eighteenth centuries. Then demand for the drug grew so great that the cultivation of

Opium pipes

Opium smokers inside China: engraving, 1843

the poppy was begun in several provinces in the interior of China itself.

At first opium smoking was a fad of the rich upper-class families in China. Gradually other people took up the habit, until the number of opium smokers was estimated as high as ten million persons, out of a total Chinese population of four hundred million. The numbers of the addicts were swelled by government officials of lesser rank, merchants, soldiers, students, servants, and even members of religious orders: priests, monks, and nuns. When addicts were without the drug, they suffered from chills, nausea, aching bones, and twitching muscles.

Opium smoking proved to be such a curse to the Chinese that the sale and use of the drug were made illegal in 1729. Toward the end of the eighteenth century the Emperor outlawed the cultivation of the poppy inside China, and in 1800 he banned the importation of the drug. Smuggling opium into China began almost at once, sometimes with the illegal assistance of unscrupulous port authorities.

When importing the drug was declared illegal, the British East India Company pretended to give up connections with it. The Company's ships no longer carried it. Instead, English vessels, called "country ships," began to appear in India's ports to pick up the opium. The country ships operated as free traders like their American rivals and functioned independently. These English country ships became the main carriers of the outlawed opium from India. Since these ships were not under the control of the British East India Company, the company could claim that it was not responsible for their activity.

Americans obtained supplies of opium from the Turkish port of Smyrna. Turkish opium, sometimes known as "turkey," was cheaper and less pure than the India product. It often was used in China to adulterate the more expensive variety.

Americans smuggled Turkish opium into China until the War of 1812 interrupted the illegal traffic. When the British swept American shipping off the seas, the Americans in Canton found themselves sitting in their comfortable hongs with little to do. There were no goods coming in to be sold, or any American ships to be loaded for home.

All the while opium from India kept coming to Canton in English ships. Outside Canton, beyond the normal patrol of the Chinese customs boats, English traders were often met by smugglers, who were called "shopmen." The smugglers came secretly to buy the drug, paying for it in silver. However, sometimes the sale of the drug went slowly for an impatient captain, or the price was temporarily low because of an oversupply. Perhaps it would be inconvenient to wait weeks or months to sell the drug. The Americans stranded in Canton by the War of 1812 proved to be a convenient solution to the problem. They became middlemen for the English opium traders, taking over the drug in wholesale quantities and reselling it at considerable profit.

When commercial activity resumed after the War of 1812, the possible profits from the drug traffic proved very appealing to American business interests. Searches were organized for new poppy fields around Smyrna. The American share of the drug trade increased, climbing to 20 per cent of the entire opium traffic with China.

The smuggling of opium led to increased corruption of the Chinese officials at Canton. Bribes became common to the Viceroy, the official representative of the Emperor, as well as to the Hoppo, the chief customs officer. Chinese officials even took advantage of their own compatriots, closing down the warehouses and then wringing exorbitant tribute from the hong merchants before permitting them to reopen for business.

The illegal opium traffic proved to be a source of great profit to almost every American trader in the Far East. There were notable exceptions: D. W. C. Olyphant Company of New York and the Nathan Dunn Company of Philadelphia, both of which firms refused to deal in the contraband.

The hong merchant, Houqua, who had dealt with many Americans in the China trade, also declared himself opposed to the traffic, even though he had personally derived profit from it.

In 1821–1822 an American opium ship, the *Emily*, owned by Captain John O'Donnell of Baltimore, became involved in a tragic controversy with Chinese customs and laws. One of her crewmen, Francis Terranova, was accused of killing a Chinese peddler woman. He was charged with throwing something to her as she stood in her little boat alongside the ship. The woman fell overboard and drowned.

Chinese law demanded the sailor's death as punishment for the alleged crime, but the Americans insisted that the death was accidental and that the death penalty was too severe. They refused to hand over the accused seaman to the Chinese authorities. The Chinese thereupon suspended all trading with American ships and firms. Under this pressure the American merchants gave up their defense of the seaman, who was taken from his ship, tried by the Chinese, and executed by strangling. The ship's cargo of illegal opium was discovered and the *Emily* was ordered out of the port without a return cargo.

Terranova's fate made it clear that entirely different

Canton harbor with view of hongs: painting by unknown Chinese artist, mid-nineteenth century

concepts of law were held by the Chinese and by Westerners. The American businessmen in Canton were greatly disturbed. John P. Cushing decided to give up dealing with opium. John Jacob Astor withdrew completely from the China trade. And, after just two additional voyages, Stephen Girard of Philadelphia abandoned his commercial relations with China.

Under Chinese law trafficking in opium was punishable by death, and the closer a ship came to Canton, the greater grew the dangers of being caught smuggling the drug. To get around the ban, a new scheme was worked out. Floating storehouses or "receiving ships" were anchored off Lintin Island near the mouth of the Pearl River, miles away from Canton. The name Lintin, meaning "lonely" or "solitary," described the atmosphere of the island. The receiving ships appeared to be abandoned derelicts. However, carefully hidden behind flowerpots set along the deck railing were bristling cannon, ready to keep away pirates and perhaps even prying officials.

Ships Levant *and* Milo *at smuggling station, Lintin Island: painting by unknown Chinese artist*

The forbidden opium was transferred to the receiving ships from incoming vessels, which paused briefly at Lintin on their way up the Pearl River. The opium cakes were packed in wicker baskets, boxes, and cases, which could be moved from ship to ship quietly and secretly.

Chinese smugglers bought orders or chits at a counting house in Canton, paying in silver. The chits were presented to the receiving ships at Lintin, and the drug was turned over to them. Chinese smugglers' boats were faster than official government vessels that might try to stop and search them. The small, speedy craft were called "smug boats," "fast crabs," or "scrambling dragons." They were equipped with sails as well as banks of oars, twenty or more to a side, which were manned by crews numbering as many as sixty or seventy. The smug boats were usually heavily armed. Chinese opium smugglers knew that if they were caught they would be sentenced to death.

CHAPTER *25*

The "Opium War"

As CHINESE OFFICIALS grew more and more disturbed by the harmful effects of opium on so many of their people, they increased their efforts to control the widespread smuggling. Western traders became more devious in their attempts to outwit the authorities. Since any ship that had touched at Smyrna would be under suspicion, shipments of opium from Turkey were sometimes sent first to an American port and then transshipped to China. Some ships transferred illegal cargoes on the high seas to hide the fact that opium had been picked up in Smyrna.

In 1838 the Chinese Emperor ordered the opium traffic in Canton completely stopped. He appointed an Imperial Commissioner, Lin Tse-hsu, with special powers to put an end to the smuggling. Commissioner Lin confiscated stores of the drug, which were valued at twelve million dollars, and dumped them into the sea. Trading with the British was suspended.

The British reacted with outrage, pulling their ships back to Macao, but they were ordered to leave the Portuguese-held port also. Moving across the bay, the British took over control of the island of Hong Kong and announced that they expected to be repaid not only the costs of the opium that had been destroyed but all the damages resulting from the loss. British warships were brought in to enforce the demand.

The Americans did not withdraw from Canton along with the British; they remained behind and carried on trade as usual. Sometimes the trade was on behalf of the expelled British—a service for which the Americans exacted a high price.

Open hostilities between the English and the Chinese began in 1839; the Chinese were rapidly overwhelmed by the power of the British fleet. The conflict has be-

Chinese opium smugglers' boat: painting by unknown Chinese artist, mid-nineteenth century

Commissioner Lin Tse-hsu: painting by unknown Chinese artist, mid-nineteenth century

come known as the Anglo–Chinese War. It is sometimes called the First Opium War, even though the treaty of peace dictated by the victorious British contains no mention of the drug. By its terms the Chinese Emperor was compelled to open four additional seaports to Western trade—Shanghai, Ningpo, Foochow, and Amoy. The treaty also provided that the island of Hong Kong be turned over to the British.

In 1844 the United States and China agreed to a treaty, in which all the terms won by the British were also granted to the Americans, except for the cession of territory. The treaty, negotiated for America by Caleb Cushing, is called the Wanghsia Treaty.

The First Opium War marked the end of an era in the American–China trade. The United States had finally shaken itself free of commercial dependence on England, just as years earlier it had freed itself from London's political rule. American shipping had established itself on a sound foundation. California, the Northwest Coast, and Hawaii had been explored and a basis established for

Hong Kong, about 1845: painting by unknown Chinese artist

incorporating the three territories within the United States.

But the days of the brave captain in his small sailing ship were gone. Trading in Canton was no longer controlled by a small group of venerable hong merchants. Now five ports were open for free trading. Instead of the long voyages around Africa and South America, the transcontinental railroad linked the Atlantic and Pacific oceans. The link between the China trade and the commerce with Europe was broken.

China also found itself undergoing vast changes as the result of its clashes with the West. Its social framework —a feudal agricultural society, ruled by a wealthy landowning aristocracy—was being shaken. The self-sufficiency it had cherished for centuries was weakened. No longer was it sufficient to ship the tea and silk that were prized in the West, accepting in return only medicinal roots, incense, furs, and ingredients for special soups. A gigantic transformation had taken place within a few decades: now China was not just a producing country;

it had become a consumer, a vast marketplace of millions of demanding customers—the opium addicts.

CHAPTER *26*

The Clipper Ships

By the middle of the nineteenth century the cultivation of tea was no longer exclusive to China. It was being successfully grown in India and Ceylon for both the European and American markets. Yet tea continued to be valuable in the China trade, although the importance of most other Chinese exports was declining. Silks and handwoven cottons were being supplanted by American-made fabrics woven on machine-powered looms. Porcelain-making had ceased to be a Chinese monopoly in the eighteenth century. Porcelain products were being made in increasing quantities as Dresdenware

Clipper ships Game Cock, Telegraph, *and* Meteor: *painting by W. N. Wilson*

Clipper ship Houqua, *built in 1844 for A. A. Low: painting by Antonio Jacobsen*

in Germany, Delftware in Holland, Limoges in France, and Staffordshire in England.

One consequence of the early years of trading never disappeared: the firmly rooted acceptance in American life of the arts and manners of the Orient.

In America and Europe the taste for tea kept steadily increasing. Ships were being built with larger and larger cargo-carrying capacities. Soon greater quantities of tea were being imported than any one locality in the Atlantic states could consume. As a result more and more of the large tea cargoes were unloaded in the port of New York. From there the tea would be routed to other cities along the eastern seaboard and even inland: up the Hudson River, through the new Erie Canal and the Great Lakes to the West.

The booming tea trade had great influence on the size and speed of American ships. Since the first teas from China always commanded the best prices, ship designers dreamed of swift boats with huge holds, outsailing all rivals in the race to reach home.

As early as 1839 John Murray Forbes's ship the *Akbar*, 650 tons, made the passage from New York to Canton in 109 days—just over three months.

The story is told that John Land, captain of the *Rainbow*, described how his narrow ship, ploughing through the sea under a cloud of canvas, had "clipped down the wind." The captain's comment has been considered the derivation of the term "clipper ship." Actually the smaller vessels built on Chesapeake Bay had already been known as Baltimore clippers. The verb "to clip" meant "to run or fly fast."

Four years later, in 1843, a new silhouette in ships was beginning to appear on the horizon. The *Rainbow*, 750 tons, 159 feet long, only 32 feet wide, with a sharp bow and tall slanting masts, covered the same distance in 92 days, even sailing against the prevailing monsoons. After spending two weeks at Canton taking on cargo, the ship was back on her way. She reached New York in 88 days, bringing with her the first news that she had come and gone from China.

The races of the American clipper ships against their British rivals were spectacular. To be the first to get tea to the market, the ships strained under every square inch of sail that could be carried.

The discovery of gold in California in 1848–1849 demanded swift passage to the Pacific. Feverish gold hunters could not wait to get to the West Coast, and the Eastern shipyards sent speedy clippers sliding down the ways. These same clippers that carried gold-hungry passengers to California often continued across the Pacific to pick up a cargo of tea for the home voyage.

For years American ship designers and builders had been experimenting, moving toward the style of the clipper ship: slender hulls, long clean lines, and overhead great billowing clouds of canvas. One of the distinguishing marks of the perfect clipper was the fine curve of the ship's bow, which gave it both the appearance and the capability of speed.

One of the first of the American clipper ships was named *Houqua*, after the Canton hong merchant, who was long associated with so many American traders. Others were given graceful, poetic names: *Flying Cloud, Witch of the Waves, Shooting Star, Flying Fish, Golden Fleece, Twilight, Gamecock,* and *Lighthouse.*

Donald McKay, the best-known of the clipper shipbuilders, had always built boats, even as a boyhood hobby in Nova Scotia, where he was born. When he went to Boston, he naturally headed for the shipbuilding yards, where he was soon busily at work as a carpenter. In 1852 he built one of his masterworks, *Sovereign of the Seas.* The day the ship was launched was declared a public holiday in Boston, with bands playing and guns firing salutes over the harbor.

Donald McKay's *Sea Witch* rounded Cape Horn in midwinter and, covered with ice, fought bitter head winds, floating icebergs, and blinding snowstorms to reach San Francisco in 97 days from New York. The passage was record-breaking. The *Sea Witch* probably broke more speed records than any other American sailing ship in the China trade. The clipper ships were prob-

Clipper Flying Cloud: *painting by Frank Vining Smith*

ably the swiftest and most beautiful sailing vessels ever built. They set speed records that have never been surpassed, and they earned fabulous profits for their owners.

For a few decades American clipper ships dominated the sea, carrying American commerce to every part of the world. The sight of the clippers along the horizon became familiar—masts taller than the length of the ship, hulls painted black, decks cleanly scraped and varnished. The long, low-lying hulls, under towering billows of sail, nosed their way everywhere. Some were decorated with wooden figureheads at the prow: a golden dragon, a mermaid, a fierce eagle, or perhaps a likeness of the lady for whom the ship was named.

The captains of the Yankee clippers were usually young men, who carried themselves with a sense of their own importance. A clipper-ship captain might be seen striding confidently along a harbor front, wearing a tall beaver hat, a velvet cravat, and shiny leather shoes. His well-cut coat might be adorned with pearl buttons; his trousers light gray, skin-tight. At his waist there was usually a heavy gold watch chain. In his hand he held an ebony cane with a shining gold head.

As a clipper ship came sailing back into her home port, the vessel gleamed under coats of fresh polish and paint. The clipper's hull, usually velvety black, was decorated with a fine gold or scarlet line near the rail. The decks, holystoned white, shone, and the brass flashed in the sunlight. As the ship anchored, the crew aboard—who called themselves flying fish men—were often heard singing.

It was a breathtaking sight, one that would linger long in one's memory. No wonder most Americans, cheering the homecoming clipper, failed to notice a smudge of smoke on the horizon, the telltale sign of the steamship, which would soon emerge to put an end to the glory of the beautiful sailing ships—and with it an era in the China trade.

LIST OF ILLUSTRATIONS AND ACKNOWLEDGMENTS

33 The Metropolitan Museum of Art, Rogers Fund, 1942

34 Drawn by Thomas Allom, from G. N. Wright's *China in a Series of Views*

36 *Ibid.*

37 *Ibid.*

38 *Ibid.*

39 *Ibid.*

40 *Ibid.*

41 Courtesy, Berry-Hill Galleries

42 Courtesy, Berry-Hill Galleries

43 Courtesy, Berry-Hill Galleries

44 Courtesy, Berry-Hill Galleries

46 Courtesy, The Henry Francis du Pont Winterthur Museum

47 The Metropolitan Museum of Art, Rogers Fund, 1965

48 The British Museum

49 *Ibid.*

50 Courtesy, Berry-Hill Galleries

51 Courtesy, Berry-Hill Galleries

52 Drawn by Thomas Allom, from G. N. Wright's *China in a Series of Views*

54 The Metropolitan Museum of Art, Winfield Foundation Gift, 1963

56 The Metropolitan Museum of Art, Gift of the Winfield Foundation, 1951

57 Drawn by Thomas Allom, from G. N. Wright's *China in a Series of Views*

59 Courtesy, Berry-Hill Galleries

60 The Metropolitan Museum of Art, Purchase, 1971, Winfield Foundation Gift Fund

61 The Metropolitan Museum of Art, Purchase, 1971, Winfield Foundation Gift Fund

62 The Metropolitan Museum of Art, Gift of the Winfield Foundation, 1951

65 The Metropolitan Museum of Art, Gift of Mrs. Mary Cornell, 1958

66 The Metropolitan Museum of Art, Gift of Mrs. Mary Cornell, 1958

67 The Metropolitan Museum of Art, Gift of Mrs. Mary Cornell, 1958

68 The Metropolitan Museum of Art, Gift of Mrs. Mary Cornell, 1958

70 The Metropolitan Museum of Art, Gift of the Bertha King Benkard Memorial Fund, 1946

72–84 Courtesy, The Henry Francis du Pont Winterthur Museum

85 The British Museum

86 The Metropolitan Museum of Art, Purchase, 1955, Winfield Foundation Gift

87 Courtesy, The Henry Francis du Pont Winterthur Museum

88 The Metropolitan Museum of Art, Gift of R. Thornton Wilson, 1940

91 The Metropolitan Museum of Art, Cadwalader Fund, 1914

92 The Metropolitan Museum of Art, Rogers Fund, 1958

94 Courtesy of The New York Historical Society, New York City

98 From Edmund Fanning's *Voyages to the South Seas*, 1838

100 Library of Congress

101 The Metropolitan Museum of Art, Bequest of Edward W. C. Arnold, 1954

103 Courtesy, Peabody Museum of Salem

104 Courtesy, Peabody Museum of Salem

106 The Metropolitan Museum of Art, Bequest of Mrs. Edith T. Pryor, 1935

108 The Metropolitan Museum of Art, Rogers Fund, 1948

111 Courtesy, New York State Historical Association

112 Courtesy, Peabody Museum of Salem

114 Courtesy, Peabody Museum of Salem

116 C. Montague Cooke, Jr. Print Collection. Honolulu Academy of Arts

117 From H. W. S. Cleveland's *Voyages of a Merchant Navigator*, 1886

120 Courtesy, Museum of Fine Arts, Boston, Gift of Miss E. F. P. Holland

121 C. Montague Cooke, Jr. Print Collection, Honolulu Academy of Arts

123 Photograph by Alfred Tamarin

125 From Amaso Delano's *Narrative of Voyages and Travels in the Northern and Southern Hemispheres, 1817*

127 The Metropolitan Museum of Art, Gift of Roland Koscherak, 1951

128 Massachusetts Historical Society

130 Gift of George R. Carter, Honolulu Academy of Arts

132 Massachusetts Historical Society

135 University Museum, University of Pennsylvania

137 Massachusetts Historical Society

140 Photograph by George M. Cushing

142 Courtesy, United States Naval Academy Museum

146 Rhode Island Historical Society, Gift of Robert P. Brown

153 From Edmund Fanning, *Voyages Round the World*, 1833

154 From *Narrative of Four Voyages, 1832*

159 Courtesy, Museum of Fine Arts, Boston, Maud M. Karolik Collection

161 Library of Congress

163 Courtesy, Museum of Fine Arts, Boston, M. and M. Karolik Collection

164 Masonic Temple, Philadelphia

165 Stephen Girard Collection, Girard College

167 Museum of Natural History, Princeton University

168 Drawn by Thomas Allom, from G. N. Wright's *China in a Series of Views*

171 The Metropolitan Museum of Art, Rogers Fund, 1956

172 Courtesy, Museum of the American China Trade

174 Courtesy, Berry-Hill Galleries

176 Collection Mrs. Francesca M. Wiig, Courtesy, Berry-Hill Galleries

177 Courtesy, Berry-Hill Galleries

179 United States Merchant Marine Academy

180 Courtesy, Fine Arts Collection, The Seamen's Bank for Savings

183 Courtesy, Fine Arts Collection, The Seamen's Bank for Savings

Map by Lucy Bitzer, from a map in Jackdaw No. A22 *The American China Trade*, published by The Viking Press; used by permission of the authors, Patricia Heard and Miriam Butts

INDEX

(Page numbers in italics refer to illustrations.)

ABOUT THE AUTHORS

Alfred Tamarin and Shirley Glubok are a husband-and-wife team who travel all over the world collecting material for their books. Ms. Glubok is the author of the highly praised "Art of . . ." series, many of which were ALA Notable Books. Her books on art and archaeology number nearly thirty, all featuring photography by her husband. Mr. Tamarin has written six books for young readers on a wide variety of historical subjects. It was during a trip to the Far East that the Tamarins began their study of America's early experiences in the China Trade.

Ms. Glubok's books grew out of her lectures at the Metropolitan Museum of Art, where she and Mr. Tamarin have lectured together. The Tamarins live in New York City.